KEYS TO INVESTING IN MUTUAL FUNDS

Third Edition

Warren Boroson

Specialist Editor
The Record
Hackensack, New Jersey

BARRON'S

Acknowledgments
Author and publisher express their appreciation to the following
individuals and companies for permission to reprint material:
Joe Mansueto, Morningstar Inc.: Morgan, Stanley & Company,
and Investment Company Institute.

All inquiries should be addressed to:
Barron's Educational Series, Inc.
250 Wireless Boulevard
Hauppauge, NY 11788

Library of Congress Catalog Card Number 96-33503

International Standard Book Number 0-8120-9644-4

Library of Congress Cataloging-in-Publication Data
Boroson, Warren.
    Keys to investing in mutual funds / Warren Boroson. — 3rd ed.
        p.   cm. — (Barron's business keys)
    Includes index.
    ISBN 0-8120-9644-4
    1. Mutual funds. 2. Finance, Personal. I. Title. II. Series.
HG4530.B67   1997
332.63'27—dc20

                                    96-33503
                                         CIP

PRINTED IN THE UNITED STATES OF AMERICA

98765432

CONTENTS

INTRODUCTION

Mutual funds are, in some ways, like insurance.

With insurance, typically, a group of people band together to protect themselves against financial disaster. Each pays a sum of money into a pool, and should one of them suffer a calamity, that unfortunate will receive some of the money contributed by all the others. The calamity could be premature death, disability, disease, the loss of a major asset like a house, and so forth.

With mutual funds, a group of people band together to make a greater profit than they might individually, and with greater safety. Because they can put more money into a fund by joining together, each member of the group can buy a piece of a wide mix of investments. Just as important, these funds are large enough to enable these people to pay topflight professionals to manage those investments.

Of course, there are risks, but mutual funds have proven to be especially suitable for ordinary people— somewhat uninformed about investing, and wary, who normally confine themselves to low-return savings accounts or slightly higher-paying certificates of deposit. Such conservative investments will not make them rich— unless they save a great deal of money—and may not even keep their assets growing ahead of inflation.

With mutual funds, John and Jane Doe stand a far better chance of making more money—not just with money-market funds (which are like super checking accounts), but with fixed-income (bond) funds, and most especially with stock funds.

Turning a profit in the stock market can be a labor of Hercules for the average individual, as anyone who invested in the market shortly before the crash of 1987 knows all too well. But by investing in a good stock

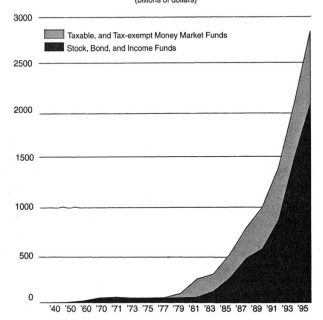

Assets of Mutual Funds
(billions of dollars)

Legend:
- Taxable, and Tax-exempt Money Market Funds
- Stock, Bond, and Income Funds

Source: *1996 Mutual Fund Fact Book,* Investment Company Institute, Washington, DC.

mutual fund, you turn the odds in your favor—and stocks, whether or not you know it, have been the surest way (apart from owning a house) for the average investor to make a good deal of money.

Virtually all stock mutual funds lost money on Black Monday. But mutual fund investors, by and large, lost much less of their portfolios' value than did most investors in individual stocks, some of whom were almost wiped out.

In short, with mutual funds you can diversify your investments for safety, meanwhile having a professional adviser decide which stocks to buy, which stocks to sell, and when. You don't need a minimum of $100,000 to qualify for these services; $3000 or $1000, or even less, depending on the fund, will do. In the average fund, you will pay your adviser perhaps 1% of your investment every year, and the total cost of your having a mutual fund may be only 1.5% of your investment every year.

Mutual funds, in fact, have a populist tinge to them simply because they give average Americans the opportunity to prosper, to raise their own and their families' standard of living.

The Simplicity of Mutual Fund Investing. Investing in mutual funds is an easy matter.

You need not pay a stockbroker or financial planner up to 8.5% of your investment for guidance. You can do it on your own, just by investing in no-load (no sales commission) mutual funds. Just write or telephone a mutual fund with an admirable track record, ask for a prospectus and application form, read the first and fill out the second, and send in your money. (But don't invest what is, for you, a large amount all at once. See Key 49, Dollar-cost Averaging.)

You may want to diversify even further by creating a portfolio of funds—some short-term bond funds and some intermediate-term, some high-grade and some high-yield, perhaps even some foreign-bond funds; some stock funds that invest in undervalued securities, some that invest in growing companies. You may want to keep investing in these funds, ideally by dollar-cost averaging. You must learn to follow a fund's performance, and calculate your profits or perhaps your losses. Of course, you also must decide when to sell any funds you own.

But to get started, phone for free mutual-fund literature.

Guides for the Perplexed. Once you have begun investing in mutual funds, or even before, you ought to read various periodicals. Good coverage of mutual funds is provided in such publications as *Barron's, The Wall Street Journal, Fortune, Worth, Money, SmartMoney, Kiplinger's Personal Finance Magazine, Business Week,* and *Forbes,* many of which have special quarterly or annual issues on mutual funds.

There are books, as well, such as the author's *Ultimate Mutual Fund Guide* (Irwin). Among newsletters are *Morningstar Mutual Funds,* published twice a month, $425, telephone: (800) 735-0700; *Value Line Mutual Fund Survey,* twice a month, $295, telephone: (800) 284-7607; and the author's *Mutual Fund Digest,* once a month, $39, telephone: (201) 444-3583.

For the industry point of view on funds, see "Guide to Mutual Funds," published by the Investment Company Institute, 1600 M Street, N.W., Washington, D.C. 20036; telephone: 202-293-7700; "No-Load Mutual Funds: Investing the Easy Way," The Mutual Fund Educational Alliance Investor's Directory, 1900 Erie Street, Suite 120, Kansas City, Missouri 64116; and Directory, 100% No-Load Council, 1501 Broadway, Suite 312, New York, New York 10036.

The Mysteries of Mutual Funds. Everyone in the investment world is forever selling, besides all manner of securities, certitude. Stockbrokers, of course, say they know all the answers; so do academics; so do editors of mutual-fund newsletters; and so do the authors of mutual-fund books.

If the stock market has gone up, for example, we hear that investors are encouraged by the narrowing of the trade deficit or even an increase in unemployment; if the market goes down, it's due to profit-taking, or increasing interest rates, or other worries. (No commentator in history has ever talked about random fluctuations.) Then there is the vast store of conventional wisdom. Small-company stocks excel at the end of bull markets. The more diversified a fund is, the better. Never buy a fund that doesn't do exceptionally well in down markets. And so forth.

This book is an exception.

There are many burning questions that this book will not answer—though you may encounter occasional timid guesses.

Despite this disclaimer, the author does believe, among other things, that

- The past performance of a fund is not a perfect guide to its future performance, but it is your single best guide.
- A moderate form of market-timing is judicious.
- A fund should not be shunned simply because of its volatility—if the investor is fairly sophisticated and the fund has consistently rebounded.
- The stock market contains pockets of efficiency, not pockets of inefficiency; much of the time, stocks are too high-priced or too low-priced.
- The absence of gold and other precious metals from a portfolio will not be sorely missed.
- The stock market bobs up and down, but over the long run it will bob further up than down.
- Over the short term, the stock market, as someone has said, will do whatever makes the largest number of people look foolish.
- Because conditions are forever changing, and human emotions are involved, the investment world will always be somewhat unpredictable. To quote the newsletter writer Cato Ohrn, "In the world of investing, water does not always boil at 212 degrees Fahrenheit."
- Finally, mutual funds are the solution for almost anyone searching for the best way to invest in almost anything whatsoever.

1

WHAT IS A MUTUAL FUND?

A mutual fund is a company that makes investments, usually in securities (stocks, bonds, and the like). If a mutual fund buys ten stocks and ten bonds, and you then buy shares of the fund, you will own a portion of those 20 securities—the amount depending on how much you invest.

The word *fund*, obviously, means a pool of assets. *Mutual* means that investors band together to buy securities.

The formal name for the most popular type of mutual fund is open-end investment company. The term *open-end* means that the company can always issue more shares; if investors flood a fund with new money, the fund can simply keep the money in cash (that is, money-market funds or Treasury bills), or buy more stocks, bonds, or whatever.

Mutual funds make a profit by charging fees to their shareholders. These fees, as we shall see, vary quite a bit from one fund to another.

The first mutual fund in this country was set up in Boston on March 21, 1924. Its net assets, $50,000, were fully invested in 45 stocks, including 50 shares of General Motors at 13¼. At the end of its first year, the fund had a mere 200 shareholders. Today that fund, Massachusetts Investors Trust, is one of the largest stock funds, with over $1 billion in assets and 85,000 shareholders.

Now there are over 7000 mutual funds—more than stocks on the New York Stock Exchange. But many people still keep their money in the bank. And many investors prefer money-market funds and fixed-income (bond) funds to stock funds.

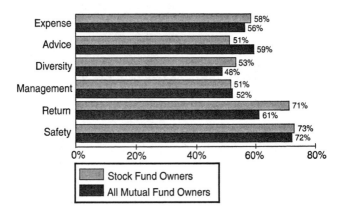

Why People Buy Mutual Funds

Expense	58%	56%
Advice	51%	59%
Diversity	53%	48%
Management	51%	52%
Return	71%	61%
Safety	73%	72%

☐ Stock Fund Owners
■ All Mutual Fund Owners

In fact, investors who gravitate toward mutual funds tend to be older—40 or so. Perhaps older people have the money to invest; perhaps, over the years, they've learned the wisdom of buying mutual funds as opposed to buying individual stocks, bonds, and other securities on their own.

True, the subject of mutual funds can be confusing. It's a broad, somewhat complex field, the jargon is often imprecise, the rules and regulations abstruse. It takes a while to understand the difference between closed-end and open-end funds, no-loads and "pure" no-loads. But everyone can do it, and this book offers the keys to that understanding.

The different classifications of mutual funds often seem fuzzy at the borderlines. Reading mutual-fund prospectuses is about as much fun as reading the tax code. It's easy to confuse the names of funds—Merrill Lynch Phoenix with Phoenix; Neuberger and Berman Guardian with Guardian Park Avenue; the score of funds with the word American in their titles.

But if you learn a little at a time—even a few keys a day—you shouldn't feel overwhelmed.

2

THE BENEFITS
OF DIVERSIFICATION

If you had bought $10,000 worth of Walbro stock on April 1, 1987, a year later your holdings would have been worth $16,800—a 68% gain.

If you had bought $10,000 worth of Digital Equipment on April 1, 1987, a year later your holdings would have shriveled to $6500—a 35% loss.

Between these two extremes, you could have diversified—bought both stocks, for $5000 each, and emerged with $11,650, a profit of 16.5%.

Diversification, in fact, should be a goal in all your investing decisions. If you put all of your eggs in one basket, and drop that basket, your nest egg may wind up being scrambled.

Of course, if you knew of one stock whose price would inexorably rise year after year, there would be no reason for you to invest in anything else.

But there is probably no such stock. Even prosperous, well-run companies—IBM, Johnson & Johnson, Union Carbide—falter and stumble. They lose enormous lawsuits, like Texaco. Or their business suddenly turns sour, as IBM's did in the early 1990s. Or tough competitors come along and steal away their business. Or their promising new product turns out to be a dud. Or indispensable company officers leave. Or the stock's price rises so high that, in response, many shareholders sell—and the price sinks below its reasonable value. Or business in general goes into a tailspin.

It's just as wise to diversify your holdings in bonds and other fixed-income investments. One reason: If you own only long-term bonds (those that will repay your investment in ten or more years) and interest rates rise, the value of your original investment will plummet. On the other hand, if you own only short-term bonds (due to be paid off in one to three years), the interest you receive may be rather anemic.

Granted, there's a rough relationship between risk and reward. The more diverse your portfolio, the less likely that you will be blessed with enormous profits. Generally, but not always. Proper diversification does not necessarily lead to mediocrity. Vanguard Wellington, for example, has done very well, yet is 85% as well diversified as the 500 stocks in the Standard & Poor's Index.

But to afford a nicely diversified basketful of securities on your own, you must be fairly rich. To purchase a portfolio of 15 stocks, you would need around $30,000. Let's say that the average price of a stock is $20. You buy 100 shares of each. (It's cheaper to buy "round lots"—100 shares or multiples of 100—rather than "odd lots.") That costs $30,000 (15 × $20 × 100). Add in commissions, and the cost rises to $31,000.

Mutual funds provide an inexpensive, nearly effortless way you can buy 30 or 100 or 500 stocks—for only $500 or even less.

Mutual funds thus offer you an inexpensive and easy way to diversify your investments—whether they be stocks, bonds, precious metals, real estate, or short-term debt instruments.

That is why, for the beginning investor, for anyone not especially well-to-do, they are a blessing.

Secondary Benefits to Investing in Mutual Funds.

- Your bookkeeping will be easier. Your fund will send you regular statements showing how many shares you own, when you bought them, when you sold them, and at what prices. This can make calculating your taxes much less painful. (If you sell, some of the larger funds will even calculate your capital gains or losses.)

4

- Your funds are "liquid." You can readily sell them and get your money out—provided you know the rules. (Some funds, for example, require "signature guarantees.")
- Some funds will do any dollar-cost averaging for you. With your permission, they will regularly take a specified sum of money out of your bank account, or money-market account, and invest it in the fund of your choice.
- Some funds will do the opposite: sell some of your shares every so often, to provide you with a regular income. (Don't ask to receive the same amount every month, or you'll be practicing the opposite of dollar-cost-averaging: selling more shares when prices are low, selling fewer when prices are high. You might ask that the same number of shares be sold, even though your income, as a result, will vary.)
- Some funds will let you invest for as little as $50, if you promise to keep putting money in regularly.
- Many fund families let you quickly switch from one fund in a family to another. Worried about the stock market? Ask your fund to sell your shares of a stock fund and put the money into a money-market fund or short-term bond fund. Think technology stocks are in the basement? Phone your family and ask to buy shares of a technology or small-company fund with money from your money-market fund. Some families even allow you to switch automatically, just by calling at any time and pressing the right buttons.
- You don't have to worry about losing your certificates, fund families usually don't issue certificates.
- Most families let you open up Individual Retirement Accounts or HR-10 (Keogh) plans, and with lower minimums than normally. Many families also offer annuities, and, if you have a lot of money, they will help manage your assets (for a fee).
- No-load fund representatives will be reluctant to give you investment advice. But as an experiment, a group of friends and I once phoned various no-load families, said that we were elderly and not wealthy,

5

and wanted to invest in an aggressive stock fund. Most no-load fund representatives said: "We can't give you advice, but if I were you, I wouldn't do it." In other words: If you have a question, ask it.

- If you telephone certain families, you can choose to listen to a recording of a fund manager explaining how his or her fund is positioned now and his or her thoughts about the investment markets.
- Nowadays, you can buy hundreds of different mutual funds from just one discount broker. Many of these are no-load funds, which even from the broker you can purchase at no fee, because the funds themselves are paying the discount brokers. Recently *SmartMoney* magazine rated the discount brokers that sell funds, focusing on (1) the number of funds they offer, (2) how well the funds have performed, and (3) transaction-fee charges. Here's how the discount brokers were rated: 1. Jack White, 2. Fidelity, 3. Lombard, 4. Accutrade, and 5. Schwab. The lowest rated were Pacific, StockCross, e*trade, Scottsdale, and Brown.

3

MANAGING YOUR PORTFOLIO

There are investors with $800,000—and more—in their portfolios who have almost no idea what percentage of their holdings is in stocks, what percentage in bonds, what percentage in real estate, and so forth.

They don't have a diversified portfolio—they have a mess.

These people aren't dumb. They have no doubt earned good money in their careers. They're just not smart investors.

Smart investors usually know, roughly, how their assets are allocated—how much of their total portfolio is invested in stocks, bonds, cash or short-term securities, real estate, and precious metals. And why. And when to consider shifting their allocations.

Building Your Portfolio. Money you have invested (not just saved" for emergencies) makes up your total portfolio. Your "net worth" includes other things you own, like cars and furniture.

Usually you won't have any money to invest until

(1) you have enough saved in a cash-reserve fund for emergencies (if, for example, the IRS claims that you erred on your tax return, and you owe a lot more, plus penalties);
(2) you've paid for the insurance you may need (life, health, disability, homeowner's); and
(3) you have enough cash on hand to pay your current bills.

The word *portfolio* can mean both your overall investments as well as your individual investment sectors—your "subportfolios." Typically, a prosperous investor has subportfolios of stocks, bonds, real estate, cash, and so forth. Your total portfolio might also be divided into your "personal" portfolio and your retirement portfolio—your Individual Retirement Accounts, Keoghs, SEPs, 401(k)s, whatever. Many people invest their retirement portfolios more conservatively than their personal portfolios, one good reason being that you normally cannot tax-deduct losses if they're in your retirement portfolio.

Every member of your family might have a different total portfolio depending on their ages and objectives. A woman in her 20s might think of stashing away a good percentage of her funds in stocks: She has the time to wait out market declines.

A man approaching retirement should typically be skewed toward income-producing investments, like bonds. At that age, most people don't have many years of a money-making career ahead of them.

The composition of your total portfolio depends on not only your age, but also on your "risk-tolerance." The less likely you are to panic and sell your stock holdings when the market has plunged, the more risk-tolerant you are. (To a large extent, your risk-tolerance thus depends upon your investing sophistication—with what equanimity you can accept the normal zigzags of the stock market.)

Your total portfolio also depends on your wealth. The more prosperous you are, the more you can afford to lose (temporarily, at least) and, thus, the more investment risk you can afford. And in the long run, the more profits you may be able to make.

Finally, your total portfolio may depend on the direction in which you think the various investment markets are heading. With mutual funds you can move your money from stock funds to bond funds to short-term money-market funds to all kinds of other funds—even real estate.

Naturally, you must keep track of your subportfolios and your total portfolio—along with your spouse's (his or her portfolio may be different because of your different ages) and your children's.

It's a formidable job. Just keeping track of the 12 to 15 different stocks needed to diversify an equity portfolio can be enormously time-consuming.

The solution, once again, is mutual funds.

For your stock subportfolio, invest $3000 and you can own shares of hundreds of different stocks—small-company stocks and blue chips, risky stocks and safe stocks. (Vanguard's Index Trust-500 Portfolio will provide you with a portfolio mimicking the composition of the Standard & Poor's 500.)

For your bond subportfolio, invest $2500 and you can own shares of 50 to 200 different bonds. (T. Rowe Price New Income will provide you with about 60.)

For real estate, invest $2500 and you will own shares of Fidelity Real Estate, which invests in a variety of real estate investment trusts and stocks.

For precious metals, invest $1000 and own shares of the Lexington Goldfund.

For a total expenditure of $9000 you can thus have a portfolio of stocks, bonds, real estate, and precious metals. (Spend more, and you can spread your net to include international stocks and international bonds.)

In short, mutual funds can readily provide you with manageable subportfolios and a manageable total portfolio.

Mutual funds can also provide you with a *managed* overall portfolio. Instead of your deciding how to allocate your assets, some funds will do everything. For openers, there are "balanced" funds, which invest in both stocks and bonds, leaning toward one or the other when their managers think the time is ripe.

4

INVESTMENT STRATEGIES

Your overall goal in making investments should be self-evident: to buy when prices are low and to sell when prices are high. To reach that goal, you must follow a tested, logical strategy—or trust to luck.

Many mutual funds buy the stocks of companies whose earnings are rising: the "growth" strategy. Value Line funds target stocks of companies whose earnings are rising, and whose stock prices are rising, too—lest no one else discover the stock for years, and its price goes nowhere. (There's a danger in being right too soon.)

Another tried-and-true investment strategy is to buy stocks that are underpriced: Bad news may have driven their prices down into the bargain basement. In any case, the assets of such companies, and their earnings, indicate that their prices should be significantly higher. This is the "basic value" approach, outlined in Benjamin Graham and David Dodd's classic investment book, *Securities Analysis.*

Unfortunately, undervalued securities can proceed to become drastically undervalued—and remain that way for years. Or a stock that seems undervalued may prove to warrant its low esteem. Battery-march, a respected money manager that seeks out undervalued securities, is famous for having bought Braniff stock *a few hours* before the company declared bankruptcy. Many an ugly duckling, it is wise to remember, grows up to be an ugly duck.

The funds that follow the simple strategy of buying and holding blue chip stocks, like IBM and GE, do well enough. By sticking with companies that pay respectable dividends and that regularly raise those dividends, these funds maintain good rates of total return.

Some funds buy a diversity of small-company stocks, trusting that the winners will eventually return far more than the losers. Diversification is the key here. While it's possible to lose 100% of an investment in a small company, it's also possible to make 1000%—or more.

Other funds keep shifting into various sectors of the economy—health care, automobiles, technology—that seem poised to prosper. Peter Lynch, who used to run Fidelity Magellan, followed this strategy.

All of these strategies make sense—and can be more profitable than just buying a basketful of stocks.

Strategies for buying fixed-income investments, or precious metals, or real estate, may be different from the strategies for buying stocks. With bonds, for example, you may want to move from short-term to intermediate-term to long-term, depending on the way you think interest rates are heading. But whatever you invest in, you need a strategy—unless your intention is to trust to luck.

You could decide which strategy appeals to you, and follow it on your own. But staying with any investment strategy when it doesn't seem to be working sometimes requires superhuman discipline. That's why you are generally better off investing in a mutual fund run by a professional portfolio manager who adheres to a particular strategy that you feel comfortable with. (A fund's prospectus will usually tell you its investment strategy.) And the keys that follow will help you decide on which funds are best for you.

Which strategy do the professionals prefer? Opinions vary. Samuel Eisenstadt, director of research for the Value Line Investment Company, points out that the growth strategy (which Value Line funds follow) tends to be profitable just at times when the "basic value" strategy is faltering, and vice versa. His suggestion: Buy at least two different funds, one of which seeks stocks with rising earnings the other of which looks for undervalued stocks.

Whether or not you follow this specific advice is a personal decision. But the overall message—that diversification is important—should be heeded by every investor in mutual funds.

5

WHY INVESTORS NEED ADVISERS

Someone hired to manage your investments is called an investment adviser, money manager, or financial planner. In the case of a mutual fund, the person is called a portfolio manager.

Ideally, as explained in Key 4, a portfolio manager will follow a sensible investment strategy, whether it be looking for stocks from companies that are flourishing, or buying stocks that appear to be selling for 60 cents on the dollar.

A portfolio manager will probably also have access to information sources that may elude you. He or she may have analysts on staff or on call at brokerage houses—analysts who dine at fast-food restaurants before deciding whether the franchisor will prosper, or who contact a company's suppliers and competitors to check on its current prosperity and future prospects. A portfolio manager can also phone, or visit with, the chief executives of giant corporations, querying them about the state of their business and their plans for the future.

Besides the discipline to follow a sound investment philosophy and better access to current, important information, a skillful portfolio manager will be relatively immune to the psychological pitfalls that beset the amateur. Among them:

Averaging down. You buy a stock at, say, 20. It goes to 15. To prove to yourself (and to your stockbroker) that you weren't a complete idiot for buying it, you buy more. "It's even more of a bargain now," you tell yourself. True, buying more might be a good idea if you were *sure* of the reason for the stock's decline—and sure that it would rise again. (At Neuberger and Berman when a stock goes down significantly, portfolio managers must either sell— or demonstrate their confidence by buying more shares.)

Being reluctant to sell losers. Selling a stock that's in the dumps would be an admission of your having made an error. Many investors can't accept that. They hold on . . . and on. Whereas many professional investors automatically sell stocks that have declined 10–15% below their purchase price. Susan Byrne, who runs the Westwood Fund, likens a declining stock to a problem child, demanding too much attention. She'll dump it from her portfolio—unless she's so familiar with it that she knows its decline is only temporary. Michael Price, who runs the Mutual Series funds, sells losers because getting rid of them "clears my brain." And his ego isn't involved: "I make lots of mistakes," he says cheerfully.

Being reluctant to buy former holdings. Investors who are averse to selling a losing stock, and thus admitting a mistake, are also averse to selling a stock, then reconsidering, and buying it again. But Peter Lynch, formerly of Fidelity Magellan, would. He would sell a stock at 50, and buy it a few weeks later, when it had climbed to 55.

Falling in love with a stock. If a stock has made a good deal of money for you, naturally you're grateful. You may even think it's "unfair" for you to sell it. And it's all-too-human to want to keep the stock, even if it starts misbehaving. Patricia Bannan, a young portfolio manager, reports that she sold Digital Equipment in early 1988, as soon as its earnings didn't meet her expectations— although DEC had made her fund quite a bundle in the previous years. "It's still a great company," she says. "But don't confuse a company with its stock."

Succumbing to greed or fear. The most common error that amateur investors make is buying high and selling low. It's a frightfully difficult temptation to resist. When stocks are rising, amateurs think that the prices will rise forever—and they must board the gravy train as soon as possible. So, greedily, they buy. When stocks are plunging, amateurs think that they'll sink into the pit—and sell in panic. That probably explains why, when anyone asks any group of ordinary investors how many have made money in the stock market, very few raise their hands.

Professional investors tend to be contrarians—to turn back when the crowd surges over the cliff. Even when the television set is set to MTV, they listen to a different drummer. On Oct. 19, 1987, when the Dow Jones Industrial Average fell 508 points, David Dreman—a famous contrarian investment adviser—bought $25 million worth of stocks. But, in fact, almost any professional investor automatically thinks of buying when the market is dropping; when the market is soaring, the professional automatically thinks of selling. Says Irwin Lainoff, former manager of the Neuberger and Berman Manhattan Fund, "When your stomach is churning, hold your nose and buy."

To sum up, what the managers of mutual funds have that distinguishes them from amateurs is the discipline to follow a sensible investment strategy; access to useful, up-to-date information; the courage to resist greed and fear; the bedrock self-esteem they need to readily admit their mistakes—and to think that occasionally they alone, among the throng of investors, may be right.

One more thing that professionals have that amateurs usually don't is time. Unlike the individual investor, investing isn't a hobby they practice in their spare moments. And unlike stockbrokers, investing isn't what portfolio managers do when they can take time out from selling.

Certainly amateurs can sometimes beat professionals. The race isn't always to the swift, the battle isn't always to the strong.

But as Damon Runyon observed, "That's the way to bet."

6

CLOSED-END FUNDS

Sometimes, a *closed-end* or *publicly traded mutual fund* may be a better choice than the *open-end* fund.

Shares of closed-end funds are bought and sold just like shares of stocks. Investors trade shares among themselves, as do the shareholders of publicly held corporations, through a stock exchange or over-the-counter.

Other key differences between these funds:

- The price per share of a closed-end fund doesn't necessarily match what the securities in the fund are worth individually. The price depends on whatever the closed-end fund's shareholders are willing to accept for their shares. And, oddly enough, you may pay less for the shares of a closed-end fund than they are inherently worth.
- The portfolio manager of a closed-end fund doesn't see any investors' money coming in or going out: buyers buy from sellers. So the number of shares in a closed-end fund is fixed. With an open-end mutual fund, the number of shares seesaws, depending on whether more investors are buying or selling.
- Because you buy or sell the shares of a closed-end investment company through a stock exchange or over-the-counter, you pay a commission to brokers who handle the transaction. With ordinary no-load mutual funds, you pay no commissions at all.

Closed-end funds have one nasty side to them. If you buy stock funds when they are first offered for sale, you will almost automatically lose money—because the fund's shares are offered at their actual value, then almost always start trading at a discount. Even funds launched by famous investment advisers, like Martin Zweig and Mario Gabelli, wind up selling at a discount.

15

Is the discount a plus or a minus? In general, a plus. Because of the discount, closed-end funds usually don't retreat so much in a declining market. Even better, some closed-ends eventually become open-end, or liquidate—usually at the instigation of their frustrated shareholders—and realize a profit when the discount is closed.

A closed-end fund enjoys another advantage: The portfolio manager need not keep any assets in cash to cover possible redemptions. Even if the market tumbles, the manager won't be forced to sell any sound securities to cover shareholders' panic selling. He or she is free to do what should be done in a declining market: Buy.

Mario Gabelli is unusual in that he manages both an open-end mutual fund and a closed-end fund. He thinks a closed-end fund is preferable for long-term investors. But if you buy and sell fairly rapidly, he would recommend buying a no-sales-commission open-end fund—to avoid the commission costs of trading in and out of closed-end funds. Studies have shown that you can make money in closed-end funds simply by buying them when their discounts are unusually high.

The *Value Line Investment Survey* rates closed-end funds on their timeliness and their financial soundness. You can consult *Value Line* in most large libraries. Large newspapers list the net asset values of closed-end stock funds and their discounts on Mondays, the NAVs of closed-end bond funds and their discounts on Wednesdays.

Closed-Ends Versus Open-Ends

Type	How to buy shares	Sales price	Shares outstanding
Open-End	Directly from fund or through a salesperson	Net asset value	Varies
Closed-End	Stock exchange	Market price	Limited

7

TOTAL RETURN

Far and away the best way to evaluate any fund's performance is to check its *total return*. Not the yield or regular income, not the distributions, not the appreciation in the fund's price per share.

What happened to your original investment in a mutual fund is your total return. A synonym: total profit or loss.

Total return includes everything—dividends, interest, capital gains, capital losses, even income from stock options (the fund may have sold investors covered calls—the right to buy stocks at a certain price). The total return is expressed as a percentage of the original net asset value (price per share)—at the beginning of a week, month, quarter, year, or whatever. A total return of 20% for a year means that your investment increased by 20% during those 12 months. In this case a $1000 investment on January 2 would be worth $1200 at year-end on December 31—if you reinvested all your distributions (realized gains, interest, dividends).

When you join a mutual fund, you have a choice. You can have all your distributions reinvested in new shares; you can reinvest just income, not capital gains; or you can have all distributions sent to you. And unless you reinvest all distributions, you won't own any more shares than you did originally (unless the fund splits its shares). Thus, if you did not ask to have your distributions reinvested, your total return may be different from the official total return. The official version assumes that you reinvested all your distributions. If you did not, your total return may be more, or less, than the official total return, depending on how the fund fared after the distribution.

To calculate a fund's total return over (say) a year, you must know not only (a) what the net asset value was at the start of the year and at the end of the year, and (b) the amount of interest and capital gains per share, but you must also know the net asset value at the time of the distribution—the price at which your dividends and capital gains were reinvested.

Most mutual-fund trackers assume that all distributions were reinvested, for the simple reason that this is what most investors do.

Here's the formula to figure out a fund's total return during the year if you reinvested your distributions:

(Year-end # of shares *times* year-end NAV) *minus*
(# of shares you owned at beginning of year *times*
beginning NAV) *times* 100 *divided by*
(beginning # of shares *times* beginning NAV)

An example: A fund's net asset value at the end of one year was 40. At the end of the next year the net asset value was 42. During the intervening months, the fund made distributions of $1.00 in dividends per share and $5.00 in capital gains. These distributions were invested when the net asset value was $41—which bought .146 shares (1.0 plus 5.0 divided by the net asset value, 41).

This works out as follows:

$(1.146 \times 42) - (1 \times 40) \times 100 / (1 \times 40) = 20.33\%$

The mutual-fund listings in most newspapers rarely provide a fund's total return over various time periods. For that, you should consult a newsletter, magazine, or one of the books mentioned in the Introduction.

8

EVALUATING FUND PERFORMANCE

It may seem obvious that, when you consider buying shares in any mutual fund, you should pay the most attention to its past performance, to its track record—to its total return over the years.

Obvious it may be, but you may nonetheless get an argument. Many academicians insist that a fund's track record is useless as a guide. The prices of stocks, bonds, and other securities, these theorists claim, are almost always exactly what they should be, because they are based on the latest, best-available information. In a word, the market is "efficient."

The only reason that any fund does better or worse than average, the academicians are confident, is its level of risk. The more speculative the investment, the greater the chance of high profits or steep losses. Thus, a fund that has been doing well, as time goes by, will become a mere average performer. A fund with a bad record will eventually pull up its record to average. Funds have splendid records or poor records only because, statistically, a few funds will always outperform or underperform the averages—briefly.

It's true that most mutual funds will, over the years, become close to average performers. It's true that many funds that are top performers one year rarely repeat the next, and that many poor-performing funds tend to bounce back. But it's also true that the funds that generally do the best have portfolio managers who scrupulously follow a sound investment strategy. And the mere fact that the number of funds with above-average or below-average records is similar to the number one

19

would expect, mathematically, is not proof that only chance is at work.

A more reasonable view is that securities prices—especially stock prices—are frequently too high or too low. After all, those prices depend on human psychology, which tends to overemphasize extrapolation from the present to the future and therefore may bid prices up too high or too low.

Many studies have shown that, over the years, a basket of stocks with low price-earnings ratios will outperform baskets with medium or high price-earnings ratios. In fact, the Value Line group has demonstrated that stocks chosen because their earnings have been growing will also outperform the market—and so will small-company stocks. Thus, it is possible to use rational criteria to select stocks that will outperform the market and to select mutual funds that will do better than their competitors.

Even granting that it's better to buy shares in a fund with good performance history rather than a mediocre or poor history, there's a sticky problem. What constitutes a good performance record?

Here is what 15 mutual-fund authorities* consider to be the key criteria in choosing funds, in descending order of importance:

*The panelists: Burton Berry, editor, "No-Load Fund X"; William F. Crawford, president, Investment Company Data; William E. Donoghue, author, *No-Load Mutual Fund Guide;* William G. Droms, professor of finance, Georgetown University; Norman G. Fosback, editor, "Mutual Fund Forecaster"; Patricia A. Ganley, former managing editor, "United Mutual Fund Selector"; Sheldon Jacobs, editor, *The Handbook for No-Load Fund Investors;* Kathleen Quigley Lantero, managing editor, Wiesenberger Investment Companies; Royal L. LeMier, editor, "Mutual Fund Specialist"; David H. Menashe, publisher, "Fundline"; Joe Mansueto, publisher, *Morningstar;* Paul A. Merriman, author, *Market-Timing With No-Load Mutual Funds;* Gerald W. Perritt, editor, "The Mutual Fund Letter"; Alan Pope, author, *Successful Investing in No-Load Funds;* Jay Schabacker, president, Schabacker Investment Management.

20

A. The fund consistently has performed better than other similar funds.
B. The fund has made enormous profits over the years—despite a few miserable years when the fund faltered.
C. The fund has consistently made a profit.
D. The fund consistently does better than the market indexes—like the Standard & Poor's 500 Stock Index.

These criteria aren't mutually exclusive, of course. A fund that regularly beats the competition (A) may have made enormous profits over the years (B), may have been a consistent winner (C), and may have done better than the market indexes (D). In considering whether to purchase a fund, you should check all of these.

Besides, the "right" answer depends on the individual investor. B is the better choice for the person who buys and holds, who doesn't panic and sell out when the market has plunged. C may be the better choice for the very conservative investor, particularly someone older, or someone who needs income to live on.

Another benchmark to consider: Has the fund's performance been in line with its volatility? A volatile fund should compensate investors for its extra risk.

As for which performance time-period to emphasize, when these same authorities were given a choice among four different performance rankings, they chose them in this order of descending importance:

A. Average 10-year record, excellent 3-year record.
B. Excellent 5-year record, mediocre 1-year record.
C. Average 5-year record, excellent 1-year record.
D. Excellent 10-year record, average 3-year record.

In sum, a fund's 3-year and 5-year records seem the most vital. But do also pay attention to the 10-year and 1-year records. And take into consideration whether, during the period under study, the portfolio manager has changed.

9

RATING FUNDS

If you're thinking of buying a fund that has been in existence for a while, you should learn its rating or ranking—how it has performed compared with similar funds over a specific period of time. These ratings are available in newspapers, newsletters, and magazines. (I'll use the term "ratings" to mean both "ratings" and "rankings." The difference is explained below.)

But the ratings don't always gibe. Even two publications that use similar rating systems, *Morningstar* and *Value Line*, sometimes rate the same fund very differently.

Rating systems. There are two major rating systems:

1. the *absolute* or *total return* method.

   You compare the total returns of two similar funds over the same period of time. You might slice all funds in the same category into five parts, and rank funds according to where they fall in these quintiles. The top 20% would get the highest rankings; the lowest 20%, the lowest rankings. (These really are "rankings," not ratings; you are simply placing funds in order of their total returns.)

   The trouble with this way of evaluating fund performance is that it doesn't give special credit to stable funds, those whose prices haven't ridden a roller coaster. One fund may climb from $5 to $15, but erratically—dropping to $3, bouncing up to $17, dropping to $9, dropping to $4, then finally climbing to $15. If you happen to need money when the price happens to be $2, you'll be in hot water. Another danger is that when the price has sunk to $2, you may panic and sell.

22

The absolute method doesn't reward a fund that has behaved itself with dignity, climbing from $5 to $15 in small, steady steps. That way, if at any time you needed money badly you could sell that fund without a big loss. Besides, the fund never sank so far that, in a panic, you might have sold your shares at low prices.

Consider, too, that Fund A could have 80% in stocks and 20% in stable, short-term bonds. Fund A's stock portfolio might climb 20% in a year. But the fund's total return would be dragged down by those low-paying bonds, which contributed to the fund's price stability.

The portfolio of a similar mutual fund, Fund B, might be 100% in stocks. Its stocks might climb 18% in a year—not as much as Fund A's. But, by the absolute method, Fund B would be higher ranked, even though its price was more volatile because there were no short-term bonds as ballast.

The absolute method ranking funds rewards aggressive funds and punishes stable funds.

2. *risk-adjusted* ratings.

With this method, volatile funds are punished and stable funds are rewarded. If a fund's volatility hasn't been matched by its total return, the fund is given a lower rating than funds in the same category whose volatility has been more in line with their total returns.

A fund that went from $5 to $15 fairly steadily would get more credit than a fund that went from $5 to $15 by way of Tipperary and Timbuktu. The fund that went up 20% with 80% of its assets in stocks would be higher rated than a fund 100% in stocks that went up 18%—although the total return of the second fund was higher.

Risk-adjusted ratings may punish volatile funds excessively and reward stable funds too generously. Twentieth Century Vista, for example, is a volatile small-company fund with an impressive record: up 14% a year over ten years. But its volatility has

23

been very high. Morningstar gives it two stars (for below average); its usual Morningstar rating is 2.5 stars. Valley Forge is a very stable asset-allocation fund with an unimpressive record: up 7.56% over ten years. It gets three stars (for average), and its average rating has been 3.3 stars.

Absolute rankings would raise Twentieth Century Vista up to the roof—and drop Valley Forge down into the dungeon.

Risk-adjusted ratings also tend to favor fixed-income funds with shorter maturities; they are much less volatile than other fixed-income funds.

A. Michael Lipper, a mutual fund authority, uses the absolute method to rank mutual funds. He scoffs that, "No one can spend risk-adjusted ratings," and he has argued that Morningstar ratings are not predictive; high-rated funds don't always continue to do well. Advocates of risk-adjusted ratings claim that investors funds with high risk-adjusted ratings can sleep well at night, and ratings are a good starting point in evaluating fund performance. (There actually is some evidence that funds with good records continue to perform well.)

Probably conservative investors should pay more attention to risk-adjusted ratings and aggressive investors should concentrate on absolute rankings.

Morningstar ratings and Value Line fund ratings sometimes differ because Morningstar does not punish funds for volatility on the way up, although theoretically risk-adjusted ratings should. Value Line does punish funds that bounce up as well as down, and Value Line staffers point to instances where Morningstar funds with low volatility ratings proceeded to stumble badly, because volatility up is frequently followed by volatility down.

Another dimension of fund ratings is the time period selected. Morningstar uses a combination of three-, five-, and ten-year records. This actually emphasizes the three-year period because the three-year record is considered in each evaluation. Value Line uses a shorter period. *The New York Times* uses three-year records, which is why its ratings sometimes differ from Morningstar's, although *The Times* uses Morningstar data. *The Wall Street Journal* uses a variety of time periods. Generally, sophisticated investors consider a combination of the three- and five-year records as the most useful.

Still another dimension of fund ratings is the question how many categories of different funds you have set up. If funds are separated into a large variety of different categories, such as 30, many more funds will rise to the top than if you placed all of them in only four categories (stocks, hybrids, bonds, municipal bonds).

An unusual ranking system is used in *Investor's Business Daily*, which uses absolute rankings and lumps all funds into one huge category. As a result, fixed-income funds—including index funds—almost always wind up at the bottom of the heap, simply because stocks usually have higher total returns than bonds.

10

STOCK AND BOND INDEXES

Indexes are models of the stock or the bond markets as a whole. If you want to know how the "market" has been doing, and how your own portfolio has been faring in comparison, you would check a suitable index.

The Dow-Jones Industrial Average of 30 stocks is probably the best-known index. It's simple and it keeps pace with more sophisticated indexes. But it exaggerates market movements, and it includes only blue-chip stocks. It's also only an average: the stock of AT&T, has the same weight as the stock of Bethlehem Steel, with is much smaller.

Standard & Poor's 500 Stock Index is the one used by most professional money managers. But it, too, is heavily slanted toward large companies, most of which are listed on the New York Stock Exchange. And because its holdings are market-value-weighted, the fortunes of a giant, widely held company like IBM can have a distorting influence. From time to time the components of the S&P change, as companies merge or fail. In all, the index represents about 80% of the market value of the NYSE stocks.

But both the Dow and the S&P give short shrift to small companies. For that coverage you must turn to an index like the Wilshire 5000 or the Value Line Average.

There are many other indexes, including the Dow utility and Dow transportation, the S&P health-care, and so forth. The components of these indexes change from time to time, as companies fail, merge, or otherwise no longer meet the criteria set by the index-makers. Morgan Stanley foreign-stock indexes include those that track emerging markets, Latin America, the Pacific Rim, Europe, and Europe, Asia, and the Far East (EAFE).

While there are hundreds of bond indexes, the best-known are the Salomon Brothers Index, the Shearson Lehman Brothers Indices, the Merrill Lynch Indexes, and the Moody's Index. But bond indexes are even trickier to use, because bonds vary by their risk and their maturities. For comparison, you must seek out a bond index that reflects the risk and the term of your own fund's holdings. Or better yet, compare your bond fund's performance against that of a similar fund.

In rating a stock fund, you should certainly use as one touchstone the fund's record vis-à-vis the S&P 500. But remember that almost all funds operate under a handicap: They usually keep some of their assets in cash or cash equivalents, just to cover possible redemptions by shareholders. They also have operating expenses, such as for trading commissions. (You yourself couldn't buy the S&P 500 without paying commissions.) Vanguard Index Trust—500 has underperformed the S&P 500 by tiny percentages in almost every year of its existence.

Besides, a fund may trail behind a suitable index but have a good excuse: It was less volatile than the index. Its price was stable, not jumpy.

11

ALL-WEATHER FUNDS

It's possible to invest in stock funds without suffering the full stomach-turning volatility of the market. You can buy shares of funds that won't fall as far, or even won't fall at all, when the market itself tumbles. *All-weather funds,* they're called.

Unfortunately, the term "all weather" is quite broad. A fund may fare well in winter as well as summer—and still have as many ups and downs as a roller coaster. A fund may be a reassuringly stable performer—and have a history of only mediocre total annual returns.

These funds may be "all weather," by the usual definition, but they may not be the best choices for investors seeking both stability and high returns.

Still, true all-weather funds exist. Certain mutual funds do nicely in bull markets and manage to acquit themselves with honor in bear markets. Beyond that, they remain stable and not volatile. And they enjoy superior track records.

One well-known example of a true all-weather fund is Fidelity Value.

Fidelity Value's total return in 1994 was 7.63%. (Total return: the growth or shrinkage of assets, combined with dividends and interest.) The market itself, as represented by the stocks in the Standard & Poor's 500 Index, was up only 1.32% for the year. Fidelity Magellan, a classic fair-weather fund, lost 1.81%. Fidelity Value has grown by about 15% a year, yet it bobs up and down only 80% as much as the S&P 500.

Here are some reasons why certain funds may do well through thick and thin:

1. Like Fidelity Value, funds may buy undervalued securities—stocks and bonds of companies under a

cloud. Such securities usually don't sink as much in declining markets because they're pretty far down in the dumps already. Generally, these stocks in such funds have low price-earnings ratios. (The p/e ratio indicates the amount that investors will pay for earnings, and thus is a measure of a stock's popularity.)

2. Funds may concentrate on stocks with high dividends. An example is Vanguard/Wellesley Income, which recently was yielding 5.5%. It concentrates on high-yielding stocks like utilities, but also searches for any that seem low-priced. When the market falls, stocks that pay decent dividends will not fall as much: The lower the price, the higher the yield—and the more attractive such stocks become. If a stock's price is $20, and it pays a $0.30 dividend per share every three months, its annual yield would be 6% ($1.20 divided by $20). If the price sank to $15 a share, the yield would climb to 8%.

3. Such funds may practice market-timing—selling their holdings when they suspect the market is beginning a major decline, or has already entered one. Example: Vanguard Asset Allocation. Some other funds practice market-timing indirectly, just by keeping more of their assets in cash when their managers can't find enough undervalued securities to buy.

4. Some funds diversify their holdings beyond just stocks. "Balanced" funds buy bonds as well, and such funds obviously are not generally as volatile as the stock market. Other all-weather funds, called *asset-allocation funds,* diversify even beyond stocks and bonds. USAA Cornerstone, for example, splits its investments among five categories: foreign stocks, American stocks, gold, government securities, and real estate.

Perhaps the term "all weather" should be narrowed to mean a fund that doesn't do badly in market declines but also (a) has a superior record and (b) isn't especially volatile.

A simple way to identify volatile funds is to check

their "betas." The beta coefficient is a number that measures stability. The S&P 500 is the standard—it has a beta of 1. A fund with a beta of 1.03 (like Fidelity Magellan) fluctuates 3% more than the S&P. On the other hand, a fund with a beta of 0.72 (Dodge & Cox Balanced) is 28% less volatile. In looking for an all-weather fund, you might consider only those with betas lower than 0.85. Such funds should be 15% more stable than the market.

Here are three funds with low betas that have enjoyed relatively high returns—funds that you can buy directly:

Fund	Beta	800 Telephone Number
Gabelli Asset	0.81	422-3554
Invesco Industrial Income	0.73	525-8085
Vanguard/Wellington	0.82	662-7447

Source: *Morningstar Mutual Funds.*

12

FAIR-WEATHER FUNDS

If all-weather funds perform well in both down and up markets, why would people buy any other kind of fund?

The answer is that all-weather funds don't always bless you with the highest profits.

In fact, many sophisticated investors prefer the more volatile fair-weather funds to all-weather funds. If you have the gumption to hold on to fair-weather funds during bear markets, or to buy them just as bull markets are getting under way, you usually will make more money than you would with all-weather funds.

Funds that definitely aren't all-weather—like Giftrust—tend to remain fully invested in stocks, holding only a minimum of cash through thick and thin. They also tend to prefer small-company growth stocks, which are more volatile than blue chips.

Volatile funds tend to bounce back with renewed vigor after a market plunge. But there's no ironclad guarantee that volatile funds will bob up as well as down.

Here is an assortment of fair-weather funds—those with high betas along with outstanding performance records:

Fund	Load	Return*	Beta	Phone
PBHG Growth	None	30.61	1.17	(800) 433-0051
Alger Small Cap	5% deferred	19.42	1.37	(800) 992-3863
20th Century Vista	None	18.31	1.36	(800) 345-2021

*Five-year compounded annual return, to 2/1/96

13

FOUL-WEATHER FUNDS

Like all-weather funds, foul-weather funds tend not to sink very far in bear markets.

Foul-weather funds come in two main varieties: very conservative and very daring.

Conservative funds invest mainly in highly rated, safe securities, like utilities, which usually neither go up much in bull markets nor down much in bear markets, and blue chips. An extreme example is Valley Forge, which has a beta of only 0.25. It's 25% as volatile as the S&P 500.

Conservative foul-weather funds do not fly very far in bull markets.

At the opposite pole are the daring foul-weather funds. These funds may sell short in declining markets, (Selling short means borrowing securities and selling them, hoping to buy them back later when their prices have declined.) An example is Robertson Stephens Contrarian.

Are foul-weather funds suitable to your portfolio? You would probably be better off buying an index fund rather than an extremely conservative fund like Valley Forge.

14

UNSEASONABLE FUNDS

Certain funds and families of funds perform miserably year after year.

Perhaps, as some academicians argue, it's just a tragic streak of bad luck, and such funds are no more likely to continue losing money than good funds are likely to continue doing well.

But it seems reasonable to believe that the portfolio managers of these unseasonable funds are just making amateurish investing mistakes, such as not diversifying, or buying high-fliers at exorbitant prices.

Certainly the Steadman Funds seem to be a cursed family, along the lines of the Jukeses.

Steadman Technology Growth has lost almost 14% a year over the past ten years. The other three Steadman funds have records almost as dismal.

According to Michael Lipper, who monitors fund records, poor-performing funds are more likely to continue performing poorly than leading funds are likely to continue performing well.

Still, while unseasonable funds have lost a good deal of money for their shareholders, their year-in, year-out disappointing records serve a useful purpose: as evidence that a fund's track record can serve as a reliable harbinger of the future.

15

HIGH FEES AND OTHER HANDICAPS

Identifying funds with good performance records is the essential first step in deciding which to buy, but it isn't the only one. Even funds with good records may have handicaps, such as high sales charges and expenses. And if you are trying to decide between two funds, you should veer toward the one with fewer serious handicaps.

A handicap is a reason why a fund may not perform as well in the future as similar funds For example, if a fund has a sales charge of 8.5%, you start off with only $915 out of every $1000 of your money working for you, whereas with a no-load fund, you would have almost every penny working for you.

Here is how a panel of mutual-fund experts (see footnote, Key 8) evaluated the importance of various handicaps:

Serious
1. A fund has a high (5% or more) sales charge.
2. The fund's performance isn't matched by the risks it has taken. While it has been unusually profitable, it has also been unusually volatile. (See Key 23.)
3. The fund has a high "back-end load," or deferred-sales charge (which can be up to 6.5% if you redeem your shares within three to five years).
4. The fund has a high 12b-1 fee (1% or more per year) in effect. (See Key 18.)

Less Serious
5. The fund has a "medium load"—a 3% to 5% sales commission.

Least Serious

6. The fund is unusually large—with assets above $500 million. Giant size is more of a handicap for aggressive-growth or growth stock funds, not for stock income or fixed-income funds.
7. The fund's expense ratio (annual expenses divided by average net assets) is high—over 1.5%.
8. The fund has a redemption fee—typically, up to 1% for the first six months.
9. The fund buys and sells very frequently—its turnover is greater than 100%. (See Key 24.)
10. The fund's management fee is over 1% of average annual assets. (This is included in the expense ratio, so it may account for a high ratio.)

In choosing a fund, you should weigh its performance record against its handicaps. Better yet, find a similar fund with a similar performance record, and choose the one with fewer serious handicaps.

16

WHAT ARE LOADS?

A load is a sales charge you must pay to buy certain funds. You usually pay this commission to a stockbroker, financial planner, or insurance agent. About 60% of all funds (not including no-load money-market funds) carry sales charges.

A fund may have different types of charges. If the charges are up front, the fund may be designated as A shares. If the charges are paid when a shareholder sells his or her shares, the shares may be labeled C shares. B shares of a fund will have higher yearly fees. Most experts suggest that investors buy the A shares if they must buy load funds at all.

Sales charges as high as 8.5% have become rare. Today most of the higher loads are 5% or 5.5%.

Over time, a sales charge that's 5% or higher can cost quite a bit of money. And it's because of the sales charge that no-load funds, on average, perform better than load funds.

A load helps cover the payment that a fund's distributor makes to reward stockbrokers for selling you their funds. (With low or medium loads, the fund itself may keep the money.) Fortunately, stockbrokers generally seem to direct their clients toward the better-performing load funds. The load funds with the most net assets tend to be those with decent records, like Investment Company of America, Templeton World, and Washington Mutual.

A load fund has a few advantages over a no-load. Because loads tend to have more assets (brokers are selling them, after all), they also tend to have lower expenses—thanks to economies of scale. And if an investor is lucky, he or she may obtain good guidance from a stockbroker or financial planner.

But as a rule, sophisticated investors never buy full-load funds. Load funds do not perform any better than no-loads; in fact, during the early years an investor is in a fund, loads perform worse—owing entirely to the sales charge.

The argument has been made that load funds can buy better research, simply because they have more money. But the sales commission, in the case of a full-load fund, does not go to the fund but to its distributor and to salespeople.

The best argument against load funds is that you can virtually always find a similar no-load fund.

Load Fund	**No-Load Double**
Investment Company of America	*Windsor II*
Kemper High Yield	*Price High Yield*
Templeton World	*Price International*

Sophisticated investors may, nonetheless, occasionally consider "medium-load" funds, those that charge 3–5%, and "low-load" funds, those that charge 1–3%. (Funds that charge 5% or more are "full-load" funds.)

Some reasons these sophisticated investors give:

1. The fund is unique.

   Example: Franklin Balance Sheet Portfolio, an open-end fund that buys closed-end funds. Its sales charge is only 1.5%.

2. The fund is new, and the portfolio manager has a glittering reputation.

   Warren Buffett is a legendarily successful investor. If he were to open a load fund, buying shares might be irresistible.

3. The fund has a superior track record.

   One investor had sworn that he would never invest in a load fund. Later he reported that he had purchased shares of Fidelity Magellan, which has a 3% load. Why? "I don't believe in fighting the tape, either," he explained. (Fighting the ticker tape means disregarding evidence—like the prices on a ticker tape.) Another load fund (3.75%) with an inimitable track record is SoGen International.

4. You invest an enormous sum of money.

 The more you invest, the more the load shrinks. If you buy $100,000 worth of shares. for example, a 5% load might fall to 3%.

While 8.5% is usually the most you will pay for a full-load fund, you could wind up paying more. A few funds also charge commissions when you reinvest distributions—dividends. interest, and capital gains. They invest your distributions at the offering price, not at a net asset value.

To determine whether a particular fund is a load or no-load, check the newspaper listings. All funds have a net asset value—what a share costs. But in the column where load funds show their higher "offering price," no-loads will carry the initials N.L. If a fund's net asset value and its offering price are the same, the fund has other charges instead of a front-end load, such as a deferred sales charge or a redemption fee.

To figure out what the sales charge of a fund is, subtract the net asset value from the offering price. If the first number is 13.47, and the second is 14.72, the difference is 1.25. Divide the difference (1.25) by the offering price (14.72), and you will obtain the sales charge: 8.5%.

17

REDEMPTION FEES

Some funds charge you a fee when you cash in some or all of your shares. Unlike a deferred sales charge or back-end load, redemption fees tend to be small, and they tend to vanish after a fairly short time.

Some no-load funds assess redemption fees, just to discourage investors who want to dart in and out.

Whereas full front-end loads are certainly a serious handicap, a small redemption fee that disappears after two or three months is negligible. So don't turn away if you see an R next to a fund's name in newspaper listings.

18

12b-1 PLANS

The infamous 12b-1 ("distribution") plan was authorized by the Securities and Exchange Commission in 1980. Named after a section of the SEC's ruling, the 12b-1 plan was apparently intended to help funds—especially the no-loads—obtain more customers, by allowing them to use a percentage of their investors' assets to bring in new shareholders. Funds are permitted to use 12b-1 fees for marketing and distribution expenses—for advertising, sales literature, annual reports, and prospectuses, and to pay brokers who sell shares.

The fees are called "spread" fees by their advocates (they are spread out over the years) and "hidden" fees by their critics .

A case can be made for 12b-1 fees. Anthony Brown, portfolio manager of the Pax Fund, a fund that makes only ethical investments (see Key 38), says that the money enables him to advertise, make the fund larger, and thus shrink its expenses. Besides, if a 12b-1 fee is only 0.25% of yearly assets, as Pax's is, it's no great handicap. You would have to keep your shares of a fund with an 0.25% 12b-1 plan for 22 years to suffer the equivalent of a 5.5% load.

But if a fee is 0.75% of net assets a year, after ten years you would have the equivalent of a 7.5% load.

Another problem is that financial planners and stockbrokers who sell 12b-1 funds obtain "trail fees" from the plans so long as their clients remain in those funds. Supposedly this is to keep the salespeople from pulling their clients out of the funds, perhaps to put them into new front-end load funds. just to obtain new commissions. But it's also a temptation for the salespeople to do nothing—to let their customers remain in funds that have turned into flea-bitten dogs.

Of course, in evaluating any fund, you should concentrate on performance. But if a fund has a high expense ratio, like 1.5% (and 12b-1 fees contribute to the expenses), it's a distinct handicap. Most of the blue-chip funds—Vanguard, Neuberger and Berman, Twentieth Century Investors, Scudder—are "pure" no-loads. And the advisers of some other funds pay the cost of a 12b-1 plan out of their own pockets; still other funds have approved such plans, but have not put them into effect.

Funds that have high 12b-1 fees cannot call themselves "no-loads."

19

NO-LOAD FUNDS

No-loads are not just ordinary mutual funds without sales charges. They seem to have different personalities as well. No-load people like to believe that they are doing society a service by allowing ordinary Americans to purchase securities cheaply, and thus share the wealth. People at no-loads are proud of their being no-loads.

However, while it may seem that no-loads have set lower minimum first investments, this doesn't seem to be the case. Of the very largest funds, Vanguard/Windsor (no-load) has a $3000 minimum. Investment Company of America (5.75% load) has a $250 minimum; Affiliated (5.75% load), $250; Pioneer II (5.75% load), $50.

Besides, it was the no-loads that took the most advantage of the unpopular 12b-1 fees. Of course, it could be argued that no-loads needed them more. But it's unsettling that many of them eagerly instituted these "hidden loads," as they have been called.

As for individual funds, it is difficult to make a case that a family that charges full loads—like the American Funds out of Los Angeles or the Putnam funds—are somehow morally inferior to no-load funds, like the Steadman group. The American and the Putnam funds have superb performance records; the Steadman funds have appalling records. Besides, some families—like Fidelity—have no-load funds as well as load funds.

Still, the impression remains that the most admirable funds of all—for performance, for concern about their shareholders—seem to include a disproportionate number of no-loads or low-loads: Babson, Berger, Dreyfus, Fidelity, Invesco, Janus, Legg Mason, Neuberger and Berman, T. Rowe Price, Scudder, Strong, Twentieth Century, Value Line, Vanguard.

20

EXPENSE RATIOS

An efficient fund, a fund that's economical, will have lower expenses. Of course, the larger a fund, in general the lower its per-share expenses—because of economies of scale.

That's why the expense ratio takes into consideration a fund's size. A fund's expense ratio is calculated by dividing its annual expenses by its average net assets.

A fund's expenses include investment adviser's fees, legal and accounting fees, and 12b-1 fees, but not brokers' commissions, interest on loans, or income taxes.

An expense ratio over 2% is considered high, except in the case of emerging market funds. Funds with high 12b-1 fees (over 0.25%), as you would expect, tend to have high ratios. (A study by Financial Planning Information in Cambridge, Massachusetts, found that the expense ratios of funds with 12b-1 fees average about 45% higher than the expense ratios of funds without such fees.) Funds with management fees of 2% or more have high ratios, too. Fixed-income funds tend to have low ratios; specialized funds, high ratios.

Here are the average expense ratios for the various categories of funds, as calculated by Morningstar:

All stock funds:	1.52%	Emerging markets:	2.11%
Aggressive growth:	1.85%	Foreign stock:	1.67%
Equity-income:	1.33%	World stock:	1.99%
Growth:	1.44%	Asset allocation:	1.34%
Growth and income	1.24%	Balanced:	1.29%
Small company	1.50%	Fixed-income	0.98%

Even though the expense ratio allows for the efficiencies of size, the fact remains that the larger a fund is, usually the lower is its expense ratio. Thus, as a fund grows larger, its expense ratio tends to shrink.

Poor-performing funds tend to have high expense ratios: Their net assets keep going down as shareholders bail out.

The argument has been made that if a fund has a consistently high expense ratio, its prognosis is poor: Eventually its performance will suffer. But this may be a case of putting the cart before the horse. If a fund does badly, shareholders exit—and the expense ratio climbs.

A high expense ratio can be a minor blemish on an otherwise top-performing fund. But again, in comparing similar funds, you should consider their expense ratios. Of course, there may be counterbalancing factors: A fund that allows a very low initial investment will have a relatively high expense ratio because it costs more to deal with a large number of small investors than a smaller number of large investors.

21

BETA: A MEASURE OF VOLATILITY

The term *beta coefficient* sounds forbiddingly abstruse, but it's a simple idea, and very useful.

The beta is a number that compares the volatility of a stock, or a stock mutual fund, with the volatility of the stock market in general as measured by the Standard & Poor's 500. The usual time frame is three years.

The S&P 500 index has a beta of 1. (Money-market funds have a beta of 0—supposedly they carry no risk of any loss of principal through market fluctuations.) A security that goes up and down 20% less than the S&P 500 gets a beta of 0.80. A stock or mutual fund that fluctuates 15% more than the S&P 500 is assigned a beta of 1.15.

While a stock fund's beta is based on what has happened, it suggests what may happen, too—how far you can expect a fund to fall when the market falls, how far you can expect it to climb when the market climbs. The beta isn't a totally reliable guide, though. Funds with high betas sometimes do poorly in a bull market, and funds with low betas sometimes do even worse than average in bear markets. But most funds with low betas emerged from the October 1987 bloodbath healthier than those with high betas.

A stock may have a high beta because there aren't many shares outstanding—it's "thinly traded." So its price swings may be wide. Thinly traded stocks also tend to be small-company stocks, and another reason that they're volatile is that little is known about them. Fresh information, or rumors, can drive their prices way up or down. Besides, such stocks are obviously more susceptible to sudden changes of fortune.

45

The price movements of international stocks and stock funds do not correlate with the S&P 500, so their betas are not meaningful. The same applies to gold and precious-metals stocks and mutual funds.

Before buying any stock fund, find out what its beta is. (Various newsletters report on the betas of the leading funds.) You may not want to reject a volatile fund out of hand, but you should know whether the fund you are buying is all-weather or fair-weather. That way, you will probably know what to expect.

22

EVALUATING RISK

Obviously, "risk" means your chances of losing money on an investment. The worst risk is losing a big chunk of your principal, or all of it.

Risk would seem to be a treacherously difficult concept to measure, but that hasn't stopped certain academicians. To them, *risk* equals *volatility*. Certainly risk and volatility are at least cousins. Volatile stocks tend to be those of small companies with relatively few shareholders, little fish in shark-infested waters, forever facing danger—from the economy, from rivals, from customers.

One way that funds are penalized for their volatility is measuring their performance against their betas. A fund with a beta of 1.2 is expected to perform 20% better than the Standard & Poor's 500 Stock Index. If not . . . demerits.

Funds may also be penalized for having an unusually high standard deviation—how much the fund's monthly returns swing up and down compared to the average price. The standard deviation measures pure volatility, not volatility in relation to the S&P 500. For example, two funds may have a total return of 18% over 36 months. Fund A may have appreciated 0.5% every month; Fund B may have had big monthly swings, down 6%, up 30%, and so forth, but both in the end gaining 18%. Fund B's standard deviation figure would be higher.

One obvious objection to using the standard deviation as a measure of risk is that stocks and stock mutual funds perhaps should not be faulted when they fluctuate upwards. Bobbing down is certainly bad, but bobbing up is kind of nice.

One mutual-fund monitoring service, Morningstar, has taken care of that objection. When it calculates a fund's risk-adjusted return, it doesn't give a fund black marks for those months when it provides a better return than you could have received from a totally risk-free investment—three-month Treasury bills. (The Value Line Mutual Fund Survey does.)

Morningstar adjusts a stock fund's performance for risk by the following means: Take a fund's total return for each month. Subtract the return from that of a three-month Treasury bill. Add up all the months when T-bills did better than the fund. Divide by the number of months in the rating period (usually 36 months).

Yet, as we shall see, even Morningstar's unusually enlightened risk-adjusted ratings seem to be severe on many fair-weather funds.

Some other objections to the risk-volatility equation:

1. The beta coefficient is measuring human judgment—how warm, or how cool, investors have been toward particular investments. It seems inherently doubtful that the beta can be perfectly reliable when human beings aren't.

   Besides, a low beta in a fund may conceal all manner of volatility—a stock that soars, a stock that sinks. Even one stock's beta may be misleading: "An admittedly exaggerated example," writes Arthur Williams III in *Managing Your Investment Manager* (Dow-Jones-Irwin, 1986), "might be a situation in which the president of a mining company absconded with $10 million in assets at the same time that a new mine worth $10 million to the company was discovered."

   Indeed, a study in the *Financial Analysts' Journal* (March/April 1988) checked how three measures of risk supported the notion that the more risk a stock carries, the greater is its return. Beta proved an unreliable guide; the standard deviation was quite good. Best of all was the Value Line ranking of a stock for safety, which is derived from a blend of both a stock's standard deviation and its fundamentals—its balance sheet and income stream.

2. For years, high-yield ("junk") bond funds fluctuated about the same as high-grade bond funds, yet the former were far more risky—which is why their

yields are so much higher. Junk bond funds crashed in 1989 and 1990.

3. You can measure volatility by comparing how much a stock or a fund's price changes deviate from the S&P 500—the beta coefficient. But you are thus comparing a stock or stock fund with a group of stocks from enormous, prosperous companies. (The use of the S&P 500 seems to stack the deck in favor of stocks and funds that emphasize blue chips.) Perhaps the volatility and the total returns from stocks and funds that invest in small- and medium-sized companies should be weighed against a more suitable index, like the Wilshire 4500 (Wilshire 5000 minus S&P 500).

23

ALPHA: A MEASURE OF RISK VS. REWARD

If the degree of risk you take matches the reward you can expect (not always true), and if a fund's beta is identical with its riskiness (it isn't), then you should be able to rate a fund manager's performance unerringly. You simply check the fund's performance against its beta. The lower the beta, and the higher the fund's performance, the better. Ideal would be a low beta and a high performance. But a high beta and a stratospheric performance would do as well.

The relationship between a fund's beta and its performance is called *alpha*. The higher the alpha coefficient, the better, but any alpha over 0 is desirable. An alpha of 0 indicates merely that the fund did as well as expected, given its volatility.

Here's how the alpha is calculated:

Let's say that, over the course of a year, risk-free Treasurys returned 8%. The S&P 500 returned 10%. Your fund returned 12%. Your fund's beta is 1.2—20% more volatile than the S&P 500.

You would expect your fund to return at least 8%—which is what Treasurys would have given you. But during the period under study, stocks returned 2% more than Treasurys. So you would expect your fund to return 8%, plus its beta (1.2) times 2%, the extra return of stocks. Or 10.4%. But your fund has actually returned 12%—1.6% more than you could have expected. Its alpha is thus 1.6.

If your fund had actually returned 10.4%, its alpha would have been 0. Average. If it had returned 8%, its alpha would have been –2.4%.

The obvious question is: Do the best funds have positive alphas?

Here are some top-performing funds and their recent three-year alphas:

Fund	Alpha
CGM Mutual	–1.9
Fidelity Disciplined Equity	–0.6
Growth Fund of America	–0.9
Harbor Capital Appreciation	–0.4
Janus	–0.7
PBHG Growth	14.4

Next, here are three poor funds and their alphas:

Fund	Alpha
Pioneer Three	–2.9
Keystone Hartwell	–7.5
Dreyfus Growth Opportunity	–7.2

Obviously, some of the very best-performing funds (like PBHG Growth) have high alphas, and all of the poor-performing funds have low alphas. But several funds with good records have been punished too severely for their recent volatility.

In short, don't be beguiled by all the fancy statistics and the two decimal places. A fund's alpha is a useful but somewhat crude guide to its performance.

24

THE DANGERS OF
A HIGH TURNOVER

A fund that buys and sells securities quickly will have a high turnover—the rate at which it changes its holdings. A 100% turnover suggests that a fund has replaced its entire portfolio in a year.

Here's how a fund's turnover is calculated:

Take the value of purchases or sales during the fund's fiscal year—whichever is lower. (If you took both, you might be doubling the rate of trading.) Exclude fixed-income investments with maturities of a year or less. (Including them would be a little unfair: They would have been out of the portfolio in a short time anyway.)

Divide the dollar value of the securities bought, or sold, by the fund's average monthly assets during the year.

Multiply the result by 100, to express it as a percentage.

If a fund never sold or bought a single security during the year, its turnover would be 0%—0 divided by any figure whatever.

If a fund bought or sold $100 million worth of securities during the year, and its average monthly assets during the year were $100 million, its turnover ratio would be 100% (1×100). That implies a complete portfolio change during the year. Of course, the fund could just have sold 10% of its average holdings ten times a year.

A high turnover—over 100%—is certainly a smudge against a fund (see Key 15). It means that the fund has high commission costs; it also may mean that shareholders have high capital gains and high taxes to pay come April 15, if the fund has been selling winners. (Many smaller funds try to play off sales of stocks with big gains against sales of stocks with losses.) If a fund has a low turnover, it is holding onto its winners—and enabling shareholders to defer paying taxes on the fund's capital gains. (You do not pay capital-gains taxes on profits a fund has made until the fund sells those securities or you sell your fund shares.)

Some funds will have high turnovers one year, low turnovers the next. But some funds always seem to have high turnovers, and the question is whether the fund's total return compensates for the high turnover.

Thus, a fund that follows the growth strategy—buying stocks that have been making money hand over fist—will usually have a high turnover. It will buy and sell as the market leaders change.

A fund that moves from industry to industry, following the economic climate, will also have a high turnover. A prime example is Fidelity Magellan. While its turnover in 1994 was a relatively low 120%, in 1992 it was 172%.

Finally, poor-performing funds also tend to have high turnovers. Perhaps the high turnover is contributing to its poor record, but more likely the portfolio manager is frantically switching from stock to stock.

True, the cost of a high turnover will be reflected in the fund's total return. But a high turnover will also affect the taxes you pay, and normally you would prefer to pay taxes later rather than sooner.

25

CLASSIFICATIONS
OF MUTUAL FUNDS

The three broad categories of mutual funds—stocks, bonds, short-term debt instruments—are too broad. Within each of these categories are many funds that are quite different from one another, and it's important to know the distinctions.

One reason is so you know what you're buying. There's a world of difference between a stock fund that sells short, trades options, and concentrates on small companies and another fund that simply invests in the bluest of blue chips, like IBM, General Motors, and Johnson & Johnson. The first, obviously, is far more risky. There's also a world of difference between a short-term bond fund and a long-term bond fund.

A second reason to be aware of the distinctions is so that you can compare the performances of various funds. If you want to know how well a fund like Acorn has performed, compare it with, say, Evergreen, which also invests in small-company stocks. Over ten years, the average annualized return of Acorn was 15.48%; of Evergreen, 10.17%.

Don't compare Acorn with, say, Valley Forge, which is in reality a money-market fund that occasionally buys a few blue-chip stocks selling at bargain prices. Valley Forge's ten-year averaged annualized return is only 7.38%. But with Valley Forge, you're getting far less volatility.

Classifying funds is tricky. A fund's prospectus may suggest one way of investing, one objective, but in real life it may invest differently. Or a fund may change its technique. A fund that ostensibly invests in small companies may veer toward larger stocks—with less potential for fast capital appreciation—as the fund grows larger.

Or the investment climate may persuade a fund to alter its objective—for example, holding a lot of cash at a time when stocks seem overvalued.

Then too, like most demarcation lines. the lines between the various classifications can be fuzzy. If a fund owns small-company stocks as well as blue chips, is it "aggressive growth" or just "growth"? If its portfolio is about half high-dividend stocks and half bonds, is it a stock income fund or a bond income fund?

Making everything even more tricky is that there are no "official" classifications of funds that all rating services follow. One monitoring service, Lipper Analytical, doesn't call any funds "total return." ("People didn't seem to understand what they were," says Michael Lipper). And it labels the riskiest funds as "maximum capital appreciation," whereas "aggressive growth" is the usual term.

Not surprisingly, the various monitoring services may also classify funds differently. Of course, where a fund is placed determines whether its performance is considered good or bad.

The closest thing to an official classification is the one issued by the Investment Company Institute (ICI), the trade association for mutual funds. Its classifications are regularly refined and expanded. Following is its list of 21 types of funds and their definitions.

TYPES OF MUTUAL FUNDS

(Source: *1996 Mutual Fund Fact Book,* Investment Company Institute, Washington, DC.)

Aggressive Growth Funds seek maximum capital appreciation (a rise in share price); current income is not a significant factor. Some funds in this category may invest in out-of-the-mainstream stocks, such as those of fledgling or struggling companies, or those in new or temporarily out-of-favor industries. Some of these funds may also use specialized investment techniques such as option writing or short-term trading. For these reasons, these funds usually entail greater risk than the overall mutual fund universe.

Balanced Funds generally try to balance three different objectives: moderate long-term growth of capital, moderate income, and moderate stability in an investor's principal. To reach these goals, balanced funds invest in a mixture of stocks, bonds, and money-market instruments.

Corporate Bond Funds seek a high level of income by purchasing primarily bonds of U.S.-based corporations; they may also invest in other fixed-income securities such as U.S. Treasury bonds.

Flexible Portfolio Funds may invest in any one investment class (stocks, bonds, or money-market instruments) or any combination thereof, depending on the conditions in each market. Because they do not limit a fund manager's exposure to any one market, these funds provide the greatest flexibility in anticipating or responding to economic changes.

Ginnie Mae or GNMA Funds seek a high level of income by investing primarily in mortgage securities backed by the Government National Mortgage Association (GNMA). To qualify for this category, the majority of a fund's portfolio must always be invested in mortgage-backed securities.

Global Bond Funds seek a high level of income by investing in the debt securities of companies and countries worldwide, including issuers in the U.S. The funds' money managers deal with varied currencies, languages, time zones, laws and regulations, and business customs and practices. Because of these factors, although global funds provide added diversification, they are also subject to more risk than domestic (U.S.) bond funds.

Global Equity Funds seek capital appreciation (a rise in share price) by investing in securities traded worldwide, including issuers in the U.S. These funds operate just like other global and international funds (see above), providing added diversification but also added risk.

Growth and Income Funds invest mainly in the common stock of companies that offer potentially increasing value as well as consistent dividend payments. Such funds attempt to provide investors with long-term capital growth and a steady stream of income.

Growth Funds invest in the common stock of companies that offer potentially rising share prices. These funds primarily aim to provide capital appreciation (a rise in share price) rather than steady income.

High-yield Bond Funds maintain at least two thirds of their portfolios in noninvestment-grade corporate bonds (those rated Baa or lower by Moody's rating service and BBB or lower by Standard & Poor's rating service). In return for potentially greater income, high-yield funds present investors with greater credit risk than do higher-rated bond funds.

Income-Bond Funds seek a high level of income by investing in a mixture of corporate and government bonds.

Income-Equity Funds seek a high level of income by investing primarily in stocks of companies with a consistent history of dividend payments.

Income-Mixed Funds seek a high level of current income by investing in income-producing securities, including both equities and debt instruments.

International Funds seek capital appreciation (a rise in share price) by investing in equity securities of companies located outside the U.S. Two thirds of fund assets must be so invested at all times to qualify for this category.

National Municipal Bond Funds—Long-term invest primarily in bonds issued by states and municipalities to finance schools, highways, hospitals, airports, bridges, water and sewer works, and other public projects. In most cases, income earned on these securities is not taxed by the federal government and may or may not be taxed by state and local governments. For some taxpayers, a portion of income may be subject to the federal alternative minimum tax.

Precious Metals/Gold Funds seek capital appreciation (a rise in share price) by investing at least two thirds of fund assets in securities associated with gold, silver, and other precious metals.

State Municipal Bond Funds—Long-term work just like national municipal bond funds (see previous page) except that their portfolios primarily contain the issues of one state. For residents of that state, the income from these securities is typically free from both federal and state taxes. For some taxpayers, a portion of income may be subject to the federal alternative minimum tax.

Taxable Money-Market Mutual Funds seek the highest income consistent with preserving investment principal. These funds seek to maintain a stable $1.00 share price by investing in short-term money-market securities (a portfolio's average maturity must be 90 days or less) of the highest credit quality. Examples of money-market securities include U.S. Treasury bills, commercial paper (short-term IOUs) of corporations, and large-denomination certificates of deposit (CDs) of banks. Because of their short-term, high-quality characteristics, money-market funds are considered the lowest risk mutual funds available.

Tax-exempt Money-Market Funds—National seek the highest level of federally tax-free income consistent with preserving investment principal. These funds invest in short-term municipal securities issued by states and municipalities to finance local projects. For some taxpayers, a portion of income may be subject to the federal alternative minimum tax.

Tax-exempt Money-Market Funds—State work just like other tax-exempt money market funds (see above) except that their portfolios invest primarily in issues from one state. A resident in that state typically receives income exempt from federal and state taxes. For some taxpayers, a portion of income may be subject to the federal alternative minimum tax.

U.S. Government Income Funds seek income by investing in a variety of U.S. Government securities, including Treasury bonds, federally guaranteed mortgage-backed securities, and other government-backed issues.

Missing from the ICI's classifications are "sector" or "specialty" funds—those that invest exclusively in, say, broadcasting companies or real estate. The ICI generally places all of them under "aggressive growth." This is probably a good idea, because it doesn't make much sense to compare the vast variety of sector funds against one another. (The ICI places public-utility funds under "growth and income," and—obviously—has a separate category for gold and precious metals.)

If you're not sure how a particular fund should be classified, despite its prospectus and its classification by the various monitoring services, check the fund's volatility. Funds in the same class tend to share similar betas. Aggressive-growth funds, for example, tend to be far more volatile than growth-and-income funds.

26

EQUITY FUNDS

"Equities" are investments where you own a piece of the action—like common stocks. They're the opposite of money you merely lend—bonds, Treasury notes and bills, Ginnie Maes, certificates of deposit. Mutual funds that invest mostly in stocks are usually called equity funds, not stock funds, because they may own convertible bonds as well, which can be exchanged for stock at a specified price.

Many investors in mutual funds prefer money-market funds and fixed-income funds to stock funds. Stocks scare many investors, especially since the crash of 1987. Perhaps it's because of their volatility. Perhaps it's because it's so easy to lose money in the market. Investors get a tip on a hot stock; they follow it for a while in the newspapers; it keeps going up; finally, they buy. Naturally, they are among the very last people to be interested in buying; now the stock doesn't just sink, but goes to hell in a handbasket.

But in exchange for the volatility of stocks, you can reap unusually high rewards—if you buy low and sell high, or just higher. The chart on page 62 shows how stocks have fared, over the years, during various economic climates—deflation, price stability, disinflation and moderate inflation, and rapid inflation. Compare the performance of stocks against the inflation rate (as represented by the Consumer Price Index), against bonds, against short-term obligations like Treasury bills and commercial paper, against housing, farmland, gold, and silver.

Only in periods of deflation have bonds exceeded the return on stocks; only in periods of rapid inflation have hard assets like real estate and precious metals matched or beaten the return on stocks.

In fact, putting everything together, stocks have been the single best-performing investment over the years—better than bonds, better than cash, better than real estate, better than precious metals. "Over the long run," write Roger G. Ibbotson and Gary P. Brinson in *Investment Markets: Gaining the Performance Advantage* (McGraw Hill, 1987), "U.S. stocks have topped the charts as the asset with the highest returns. One dollar invested in 1789 would have earned over an 8% annual return, and the money would have doubled roughly every nine years. Through the magic of compounding, investors would have made almost 5 million times their money in such equities."

Lessons: Stay in the market. Don't plunge into the market in any particular year: If you had invested in stocks at the beginning of 1929, you might not have shown a gain until 1937—eight years later.

ANNUAL RATES OF RETURN UNDER VARIOUS ECONOMIC CONDITIONS

	CPI**	Stocks	Bonds	T-Bills†	Housing	Farmland	Gold	Silver
Deflation								
1871–1896	-1.5%	5.5%	6.4%	5.4%	N/AV	N/AV	*	-6.8%
1892–1895	-3.3	-2.5	5.1	4.1	1.5%	N/AV	*	-8.0
1919–1922	-2.0	5.0	4.2	6.7	1.0	-12.1%	*	-18.2
1929–1932	-6.4	-21.2	5.0	3.0	-3.9	-12.3	*	-19.8
Average	-3.3	-3.3	5.2	4.8	-0.4	-12.2		-13.2
Price Stability								
1896–1900	0.3	26.1	3.3	3.3	0.0	9.3	*	-1.0
1921–1929	-1.3	20.2	6.4	5.4	4.4	-2.8	*	-3.3
1934–1940	1.0	12.2	6.2	0.7	7.2	3.9	6.3%	1.0
1952–1955	0.3	24.5	3.5	1.5	4.5	6.5	*	2.1
Average	0.1	20.8	4.9	2.7	4.0	4.2		-0.3
Disinflation & Moderate Inflation								
1885–1892	0.0	4.5	4.4	5.1	N/AV	N/AV	*	-4.5
1899–1915	1.3	8.2	4.1	5.3	5.7	N/AV	*	-0.5
1942–1945	2.5	26.1	4.5	0.9	10.0	18.1	*	-3.3
1951–1965	1.6	16.5	2.2	3.5	5.5	6.7	*	3.0
Average	1.4	13.8	3.8	3.7	5.3	6.2	-0.5	-1.3
1981–1985	3.8	20.2	22.0	9.6	5.3	-8.1		-16.4
Rapid Inflation								
1914–1919	13.3	11.6	2.1	4.7	17.5	14.7	*	15.5
1940–1947	6.8	12.3	2.6	1.0	12.2	18.5	*	8.6
1949–1951	5.8	24.8	0.9	2.3	10.2	21.7	*	20.5
1965–1971	4.0	6.4	6.1	6.8	10.3	12.7	31.6	23.7
1971–1981	8.3	5.8	3.8	8.8	10.3	14.6	28.0	21.5
Average	8.3	12.2	3.1	4.7	12.1	16.4	11.9	18.0

*Under government regulation, the U.S. market price of gold did not change during this period.
** Consumer Price Index
†U.S. T-Bills and Commercial Paper
Averages do not double count overlaps, N/AV = Not Available
Source: Morgan Stanley Research

27

U.S. STOCK PORTFOLIOS

The stock funds you own shouldn't be peas in a pod. Your fund portfolio shouldn't concentrate on stocks in the same industry (like health care or technology), or stocks of the same size, or stocks with similar characteristics (earnings growing rapidly, for instance). If that were the case, your portfolio would be monolithic. Your funds would behave almost as if they were just one fund. They would go up together—and they would go down together.

If your funds are different from one another, your portfolio overall should be relatively stable. If some funds are down, others may be up.

That's why your portfolio normally should not consist of funds that buy only the stocks of big companies—"big caps." While large-company stocks are less volatile than small-company stocks, small companies tend to do better over the years, although their glory days tend to come in occasional, erratic spurts. Large-company stocks and small company stocks also may alternate their time in the sun. When big caps do well, small caps may be in the dumps—and vice versa.

The same is true of the two key investment strategies: buying the stocks of growing companies and buying the stocks of undervalued companies. Growth stocks and value stocks tend to excel at different times. (To distinguish growth from value stocks, Morningstar uses price-book ratios and price-earnings ratios. U.S. funds are measured relative to the Standard & Poor's 500 Stock Index; foreign funds are measured against foreign index funds, using price to cash flow rather than price-earnings ratios.)

The ordinary classifications of mutual funds don't always tell whether a fund follows the "growth" or "value" strategy. "Growth" funds in general, for example, may follow either the growth or the value strategy.

To sum up: Your fund portfolio should contain funds that buy big-company stocks as well as small-company stocks, funds that buy growth stocks as well as value stocks.

Some funds are in between; they may buy middle-sized companies. (Morningstar defines small as a market capitalization of less than $1 billion; medium, between $1 billion and $5 billion; and large, over $5 billion. Capitalization is price times shares outstanding.)

A well-diversified portfolio will have at least four types of U.S. stock funds: large-company growth, large-company value, small-company growth, and small-company value. (Granted, some funds may move into different boxes as time goes by. For example, successful small or mid-sized funds may move up as money pours in and they must buy larger companies.)

For further diversification of a large portfolio, you might go into blend funds and mid-cap funds. Otherwise, you might use blend and mid-cap funds when you cannot find funds in the other four categories that you admire.

Funds in the top left of the "style box" (see p. 65) are the safer ones, simply because big-company stocks tend to be safer than small-company stocks and value stocks tend to be safer than growth stocks (their prices are presumably already on the low side). So, an older, more conservative person might have more funds, or more money, in the northwest section of the style box, whereas a more aggressive person might have more funds, or more money, in the southeast section of the style box. As people age, they might shift their portfolios from southeast to northwest.

To launch a portfolio, someone inexperienced might begin with a large value fund, just to get accustomed to stock market volatility in small doses.

To build up a portfolio of good no-load funds, someone might consider funds like these in the different categories·

large-cap value: Dodge & Cox Stock, $2500 minimum, 800-621-3979

mid-cap value: Oakmark, $2500 minimum, 800-625-6275

small-cap value: Fidelity Low Priced Stock, 3% sales charge, $2500 minimum, 800-544-8888

large-cap blend: Scudder Growth and Income, $1000, 800-225-2470

mid-cap blend: Neuberger & Berman Partners, $1000, 800-877-9700

small-cap blend: Baron Growth and Income, $2000, 800-992-2766

large-cap growth: Janus Mercury, $1000, 800-525-8085

mid-cap growth: T. Rowe Price Mid-Cap Growth, $2500, 800-638-5660

small-cap growth: Kaufmann, $1500, 800-237-0132

If you choose to have only one or two funds rather than a somewhat complex diversified portfolio, you might choose an asset-allocation fund, an index fund, or a "life-style" fund—one well-diversified fund that can serve as the foundation of your entire portfolio.

Equity Style Box

Investment Style

Value	Blend	Growth
Large-cap Value	Large-cap Blend	Large-cap Growth
Mid-cap Value	Mid-cap Blend	Mid-cap Growth
Small-cap Value	Small-cap Blend	Small-cap Growth

28

FOREIGN STOCK PORTFOLIOS

While foreign funds have not performed well in recent years, the sound argument is made that they help to diversify a portfolio. Foreign stocks may go up while U.S. stocks go down. Besides, exposure to foreign stocks increases your chances of doing better than you would have with only domestic funds.

Foreign funds carry extra risks, unfortunately—political risks as well as currency risks. If the dollar gains in value vis-à-vis a particular foreign currency, your investment abroad will suffer, unless the risk has been "hedged" (in effect, insured against). Other countries' accounting standards may also be less trustworthy than ours.

To construct a portfolio of foreign funds, the Value Line Mutual Fund Survey suggests that you consider four types:

1. Multi-country, multi-region funds, which invest mainly in large-company stocks anywhere outside the United States;
2. Single-country, single region funds, which are much riskier;
3. Small-cap funds; and
4. Emerging-markets funds.

Value Line suggests that a "moderate" international stock-fund portfolio would look like this:

- multi-country, multi-region (40%)
- single-country, single-region (20%)
- foreign small company (20%)
- emerging markets (20%)

Some moderate investors might not want to own any foreign single-country, single-region mutual funds. In any case, many multi-country funds have a sizable exposure to emerging markets. In general, there's agreement that a person needs a ten-year time horizon to invest safely in emerging market funds.

Value Line recommends, among other foreign funds, Managers International Equity Fund (800-835-3879) for a multi-country, big-cap fund and Acorn International (800-922-6769) for a foreign small-company fund.

Other foreign no-load funds with good records include Founders Passport, Hotchkis and Wiley International, Janus Overseas, T. Rowe Price International, and Vanguard International Growth.

The conventional wisdom is that a well-diversified portfolio might have 10% to 30% in foreign funds.

29

SPECIALTY/SECTOR FUNDS

These are a hybrid between individual stocks and typical mutual funds. They are more diversified than the former, less diversified than the latter. They are variously called specialty funds, single-industry funds, and sector funds, but what they do is concentrate their investments in a rather narrow area.

Not considered specialty or sector funds are those that invest only in small-company stocks, or in "socially responsible" companies, or in a variety of investments that mirror an index, or in the securities of only one foreign country.

As for funds with a narrower focus, perhaps they should be segregated according to the amount of their diversification, with the broader ones being called specialty funds and the concentrated ones, sector funds. Specialty funds seem able to offer almost the diversification of normal mutual funds. Among the specialty funds are those that invest in a variety of real estate (real estate investment trusts and real estate stocks) or in the stocks of companies in one region of the United States.

Among the sector funds are those that invest in just agriculture, chemicals, health care, precious metals, insurance companies, technology. brokerage firms, or the entertainment industry. Fidelity Investments pioneered in offering a whole panoply of sector funds in 1981, and the family now offers a wide variety of sector funds, from energy to utilities. Invesco and Vanguard also now offer a series of sector funds.

For most investors, sector funds—as opposed to specialty funds—should probably be off-limits. Such funds tend to be extremely volatile, simply because they don't have the diversification of normal mutual funds. (While funds that invest in utilities seem to qualify as sector funds, they probably should be considered specialty funds because of the basic conservatism and stability of utilities stocks.)

Probably sector funds are best left to

(1) very sophisticated investors, who believe that they can figure out in advance which industries will flourish for a while;

(2) investors who prefer owning stocks, not funds, but want more stability in their stock portfolios; and

(3) long-term investors who are of a mind that certain sectors will perform exceptionally well over the long run—health care, for example.

30

FIXED-INCOME FUNDS

In recent years, corporate bonds, municipal bonds, Ginnie Maes, U.S. Treasurys, and other fixed-income investments have become almost as volatile as stocks.

Buying fixed-income investments, like corporate bonds, is no longer a simple matter, either. The difference between what two different brokers may charge in commissions can be enormous. So can the "spread"—the difference between the "wholesale" price the brokerage firm pays for a bond and the "retail" price it charges you. You must also pay attention to "call" provisions (see below), credit ratings, and maturities.

You could, of course, just buy bonds of blue-chip companies, or high-rated municipals, or U.S. Treasurys—if you have $5000 or $10,000—and hold on until the securities mature, hoping that inflation does not erode your principal. But you could make more money with a diversified portfolio that includes lower-rated bonds. And you'll be more insulated from fluctuating interest rates with a portfolio that includes bonds of different maturities. Finally, you can invest with only $500 or so. Hence, the case for using mutual funds.

In general, fixed-income investments are safer than investments in equities, or stocks. When you lend money by purchasing bonds or CDs, you're less likely to lose your principal, just as you're less likely to have your principal appreciate much before the loan comes due. (But in the world of investing, there are almost always exceptions. A low-rated bond may not be as safe as a blue-chip stock; long-term bonds—those that mature in ten years or more—may be more volatile than utilities or other conservative stocks.)

All loans are called "fixed-income" investments, though many yields are not really carved in stone. The interest rates on a money-market fund fluctuate from week to week; some notes have floating rates; even the yield on a unit investment trust (see below) can change as bonds are retired.

When you put money into mutual funds that invest primarily in bonds and other debt instruments, you always assume certain risks:

1. Rising interest rates—the longer a bond's maturity, the more the principal will erode if interest rates climb. A bond worth $1000 and paying 8% will be worth less on the market it interest rates rise to 9%. If interest rates remain high, the bond won't be worth the full $1000 until its maturity date. A better measure of a bond or fund's sensitivity to changes in interest rates is its "duration," which takes into consideration interest payments.
2. Creditworthiness—the corporation may get into trouble (lawsuits, poor earnings, high debts), and its bonds may lose favor with investors, or even go into default.
3. Call provisions—if a bond can be called in at the end of ten years. and interest rates have declined, the issuer will pay off the bondholders (usually at a small premium) and leave them with the task of finding other bonds with high yields even though interest rates are low.
4. "Event" risk. A company may become the subject of a takeover bid or leveraged buyout involving additional debt, so that its existing bonds are downgraded.

The safest bond funds, obviously, are those that hold bonds with the shortest maturities, the highest ratings, and the strongest call protection. Most Treasurys cannot be called, and municipals rarely. Short-term bonds are generally considered those with maturities of less than three years; intermediate term, three to ten years; long-term, over ten years.

When you buy a standard open-end bond fund, you're sacrificing the assurance of getting your full principal back. The fund manager buys and sells bonds before maturity, perhaps even retreating entirely into cash, depending on where he or she thinks interest rates are going. But you gain the possibility of a higher yield and even capital gains. With an open-end bond fund, the minimum may be as low as $250, and you can sell at any time. Many funds have no sales charges. And any diversified basket of bonds can include some high-yield varieties, with the diversification protecting the fund in case of an occasional default.

You can buy funds based on their maturities or on the creditworthiness of their holdings. But you may have to phone a fund to learn the average maturity of its holdings or the grades of their securities—the name sometimes provides no clue, and the prospectus gives the fund lots of leeway. You can also invest in a flexible fund, where the manager can decide which maturities and types of securities to emphasize.

Just don't make the horrendous mistake of buying a bond fund simply because of its higher yield, which can be a trap. Some funds with high yields have been losing principal. In one recent year, one bond fund had a yield of 14.5% and a total return of –6.4%, whereas another had a yield of 12.9% and a total return of 3%. You would have been 9.4 percentage points better off in the second, despite its lower yield.

By and large, you will be better off with a fund with a large asset base. It will have the clout to obtain the better securities, as well as the money to be widely diversified. Also pay attention to fund expenses. Because the yields from different bond funds aren't usually wide, funds that keep expenses low are likely to be among the leaders. Vanguard High Yield's expense ratio is usually around 0.34%, First Investors for Income, around 1.22%.

A *unit trust* will give you good diversification and the benefits of professionals picking the bonds that go into the trust. But there's little flexibility, since the trust holds the bonds until maturity, paying you interest over 1 to 30 years (depending on the trust) and then returning your principal.

31

FIXED-INCOME PORTFOLIOS

Matching the style box for stocks is a style box for fixed-income investments, which is printed on p. 74. Here, the two chief dimensions are credit quality (high, medium, low), and maturity (short, intermediate, and long).

The danger areas are low-quality, long-maturity; the safer areas, high-quality, short maturity.

An investor seeking income might begin by purchasing the less risky bond funds (short-term, high quality), then the more risky ones (intermediate-term, low quality). The conventional wisdom is that ordinary investors should be wary of long-term bonds, and if they are willing to entertain risk, they should invest in stocks instead.

A flexible-bond fund might also be appropriate for a portfolio, a fund that buys what the manager believes the best securities happen to be at any time. A good flexible-bond fund, for example, has been Loomis-Sayles Bond, telephone: (800) 633-3330.

An attractive all-purpose fixed-income fund is T. Rowe Price Spectrum Income, which owns a variety of other T. Rowe Price fixed-income funds—from Treasuries to junk. It also may have as much as 20% of its portfolio in high-dividend paying stocks. The minimum is $2500, telephone: (800) 638-5660.

Because the Vanguard Group has such low expenses, it's a good idea to compare any fixed-income fund you're considering buying with a similar fund from the Vanguard family.

Here are some fixed-income funds with good track records:

Fund	800 Telephone Number
Strong Government	368-1030
Harbor Bond (corporate)	422-1050
Northeast Investors Trust (low-rated bonds)	225-6704
Vanguard Municipal Intermediate	662-7447

Maturity

Short	Intermediate	Long	
			Quality — **High**
			Medium
			Low

32

MONEY-MARKET
FUNDS

Money-market mutual funds are like checking accounts—but, in most ways, much better.

Whatever money you put into such a fund, you will receive back. It's risk-free. (Well, almost risk-free—read on.) If you invest $1000, you will receive your $1000 back—tomorrow or 5 or 50 years down the road, at your choice. When professional investors talk of keeping some of their assets in "cash," they usually mean money-market funds.

Your $1000 has bought 1000 shares—the price of shares of almost all money-market funds is kept at $1. Meanwhile, your money earns interest—but the interest rate varies from week to week. These rates have almost always been higher than the rates you can receive from passbook savings accounts, NOW or super-NOW accounts, or money-market deposit accounts (what commercial banks and savings and loan associations call their own money-market funds). True, you may receive a higher interest rate if you invest in a six-month certificate of deposit, but you usually can't withdraw the money, without penalty, for six months.

Most money-market funds will provide you, free, with checks to use against your deposits. The minimum amount you can write may be $250 or $500. Most funds, again, don't set a limit on how many checks you can write, free of charge, within any time period. (Most money-market deposit accounts set a limit—such as three checks a month.) There's also a minimum amount you need in order to set up a money-market fund: usually $250 to $500.

When you shop for a money-market fund, focus on the interest rate—but also pay attention to the details about check-writing privileges and minimums. And keep in mind that, for absolute safety, a bank's money-market deposit account has an advantage: Government agencies insure the accounts at most banks and S&Ls for up to $100,000 each. A money-market mutual fund is usually not insured, though these funds invest in short-term U.S. government notes and bills; other very safe securities like $100,000-and-up ("jumbo") certificates of deposit offered by banks; and commercial paper—short-term obligations issued by corporations.

The first money-market fund—the Reserve Fund—was launched in 1972. Before then, only the rich could afford to invest huge amounts—$100,000 and more—in short-term debt instruments to capture high interest, while retaining their liquidity (ready access to their money) and safety of funds. Money-market funds have allowed ordinary investors to obtain high yields on their deposits, too, at the same time that their deposits remained accessible. Again, mutual funds have served as a means of democratizing the investment process.

These debt instruments cannot extend more than an average of 90 days. Thus, the fund's principal is relatively stable: Normally you won't lose much if you had a 60-day note, interest rates rose, and you were forced to sell your note before 60 days had elapsed.

What money-market funds do to keep their principal absolutely unchanging is to vary the interest rate that shareholders receive. The rate changes from week to week, though usually these variations are tiny. Whereas your shares always should have a value of $1, your current yield may be 4.7% one week, 4.68% another week. And if interest rates start climbing, your yield will go up rather quickly, too.

Indeed, back in 1981, when inflation was raging, some funds were paying almost 18% a year. By the same token, when interest rates decline, money-market funds aren't especially desirable; at one point in the 1980s, money-market funds were paying the same rates you would get from a bank's passbook savings account.

Money-market funds can also invest in short-term tax-exempt securities issued by states, cities, and public authorities. Your interest will be less, but it will escape federal taxation. If you invest in a fund that buys only the short-term securities issued in your home state, your interest may escape both federal and state taxes. This is, of course, tempting for taxpayers who live in states with fairly high tax rates. Funds may also invest entirely in short-term Treasury securities, which are of course backed by the full faith and credit of the U.S. government, and which are also exempt from state taxes in most states.

Many investors mistakenly think that the yields on different money-market funds are so close that it isn't worth the bother of shopping around. While this may be true if you have only a few hundred dollars, it isn't true if you're handling sizable amounts of money for good periods of time. Year after year, certain money-market funds pay higher rates than others. For example, if you invest $5000 in a fund yielding 5.25% a year, your investment would grow to $8423 over ten years. If the fund's yield was 6.25% a year, your $5000 would grow to $9296. The difference is $873, which would have gone a long way toward paying the taxes due on your fund's earnings. (See the chart on p. 78.)

A fund can boost its yield by extending the maturity of the debt instruments in its portfolio or by buying Eurodollars, say, or low-grade commercial paper. Eurodollars are deposits in foreign branches of American banks. In an emergency—like a war—these deposits may be frozen. Commercial paper involves short-term loans to companies that need cash temporarily. Low-grade paper—issued by not-especially-prosperous companies—carries a small amount of risk.

If you're very worried about safety, stick with funds that have net assets of $100 million or more; that buy debt with average maturities in line with those of other funds; and that do not buy Eurodollars or non-prime paper. Or just invest in money-market funds that buy government securities.

But bear in mind that the last time any money-market mutual fund lost ordinary investors any money was back in 1978. The manager of a tiny fund, First Multifund for Income, expected that interest rates would decline, so he extended his loans' average maturities to 650 days. Interest rates climbed. The fund's price per share fell below $1, to 93 cents. The fund liquidated, and its investors lost 7% of their principal. (Of course, for a time, the fund paid unusually high rates—because it had become, in effect, a short-term bond fund.)

In 1994, a small money-market fund in Colorado for institutional investors lost money.

The Difference that 1% Makes

To figure out how much more you will earn on a money-market mutual fund that pays 1% or 2% more per year than another fund, check the table below. The table uses investments of $3000 and $5000 as examples. Thus, $3000 invested for 15 years at 5.25% will give you $6560. But $3000 invested at 6.25% will give you $7605—a difference of $945.

Yield	Amount	1 Year	3 Years	5 Years	10 Years	15 Years
5.25%	$3,000	$3,161	$3,508	$3,894	$5,054	$6,560
	5,000	5,268	5,847	6,490	8,423	10,933
6.25%	3,000	3,192	3,613	4,091	5,578	7,605
	5,000	5,320	6,022	6,818	9,296	12,676

33

REAL ESTATE FUNDS

Real estate is a keen rival of a diversified basketful of common stocks. Well-chosen real estate has kept pace with the appreciation of stocks—without their volatility. The drawback of most real estate investments, of course, is their lack of liquidity. You can't quickly sell vacant land, a house, an industrial property, or a real estate limited partnership.

Mutual funds may not be the best way to buy real estate, even though they do provide liquidity. Instead, you can buy real estate investment trusts—which are sold like stocks on exchanges. You will get a diversified selection of properties, mortgages, or both. The *Value Line Investment Survey* rates various REITs for safety and timeliness and also gives a periodic review of the industry. There are also many local, regional, and national limited partnerships that invest in real estate. REITs may be preferable, as a rule. They are much more liquid. And it's easier to choose a good REIT than a good limited partnership.

A few mutual fund families have begun offering funds that concentrate on real estate. Fidelity Real Estate invests in REITs as well as in stocks of companies directly or indirectly in real estate. These funds have not been paragons of performance. They may need time to prove themselves. And the question has been raised about the wisdom of investing in real-estate ventures via mutual funds versus investing in the variety you can obtain from a REIT. T. Rowe Price and Vanguard, after all, are rather smart mutual-fund companies, yet they chose the REIT route, not a mutual fund.

A final possibility: asset-allocation funds that include real estate in their holdings. Among them are USAA Cornerstone (no-load; 800-382-8722; $3000 minimum).

34

PRECIOUS METALS FUNDS

"Become a bullionaire!" proclaimed a circular mail around the country. And these days even many shrewd investment advisers urge that everyone have 5% to 15% of their portfolios in gold, or in precious metals in general.

But many other professional investors are dubious. Over the long run, gold has not fared very well. Lexington Goldfund's average annualized return over the past ten years has been a mere 8.67%. And that's one of the better precious-metals funds.

To invest in gold, you can buy the bullion itself; you can buy gold certificates from a dealer, stockbroker, or banker; you can buy coins; or you can buy the stocks of gold-mining companies. Generally, these stocks climb faster when gold is in demand—and sink faster when demand falters. South African mining companies pay higher dividends than domestic or other foreign companies, but their stocks are risky because of the country's racial troubles.

Finally, you can buy gold through mutual funds. Some invest exclusively in gold-mining companies; others invest in gold bullion as well, which may give a portfolio more stability; still others invest in silver and platinum, thus providing more diversity.

Investors interested in owning gold might be best advised to look for a fund with a good record, a fund that can invest in bullion, silver, and platinum, and that invests in both South Africa and in other countries.

Probably an even better way to invest in gold is via an asset-allocation fund, such as USAA Cornerstone.

35

FUND FAMILIES

There are benefits to buying funds from only one mutual family. You'll know the rules—such as what minimum first investments are and how to withdraw money. It will be easy to buy new funds, or to shift around from one fund to another. Your paperwork will be a snap. If you buy load funds in one family, through a stockbroker or financial planner, you can transfer from one fund to another without paying new sales charges.

On the other hand, if you remain within one family you won't have access to some excellent "orphan" families, like the SoGen Funds or Kaufmann. Besides, fund families tend to have similar investment strategies. The Neuberger & Berman funds, Mutual Series, Scudder, and Dodge & Cox tend to buy undervalued stocks; Janus, Twentieth Century, American, Strong, and Founders tend to buy the stocks of growing companies.

These are the families that the newsletter, *The Mutual Fund Forecaster*, has rated (March 1996) as the very best, based on their individual funds' risk-adjusted ratings (where funds are punished for volatility, rewarded for stability):

Alger, Columbia, Fidelity, First American, Founders, General Electric, Janus, MAS, Morgan Stanley, Neuberger & Berman, One Group, T. Rowe Price, Scudder, SteinRoe, Strong, Twentieth Century, Vanguard, and Warburg Pincus.

The three very top-rated funds are T. Rowe Price, Fidelity, and Vanguard.

The following are the lowest-rated funds: Eaton Vance, Enterprise, First Investors, IDS (American Express), John Hancock, Kemper, Keystone, Lord, Abbett, Merrill

Lynch, Nicholas Applegate, Oppenheimer, PaineWebber, Phoenix, Rembrandt, Sentinel, Smith Barney, SunAmerica, United, and United Services.

By and large, brokerage-firm families wind up at the bottom of the heap. Perhaps it's because they have so many drop-in customers that their managers feel that they need not work hard to improve the performances of their funds. They're like restaurants in airports: They'll have customers whether the food they serve is good or not, so the food tends not to be top-notch.

Only families with at least five stock funds were rated, which is why families like the Mutual Series funds and Dodge & Cox don't appear on the list. The 93 funds were ranked in five sections; 20% wound up among the top, 20% at the bottom.

Warning: Certain families of funds that everyone thought were top-notch five years ago have since lost their glittering reputations. The Phoenix funds, for example, are no longer considered the fine family they once were. On the other hand, some families once dismissed as mediocre have since climbed close to the top, an example being Putnam.

36

NONDIVERSIFIED FUNDS

It will surprise even serious students of mutual funds that some of them are nondiversified. As defined by the Securities and Exchange Commission, to be classified as "diversified" a fund must keep 75% of its assets diversified, so that no more than 5% of its assets are in the securities of one company.

But funds can obtain permission to be labeled "nondiversified," in which case only 50% of their assets need be diversified, and up to 25% of their net assets can be in a single company. (Many new funds begin as nondiversified, just to obtain time to build up their holdings.)

Running a nondiversified fund, portfolio managers need not spread themselves too thin. Some nondiversified funds have as few as eight or ten stocks. The manager can concentrate his or her attention on a limited basketful of securities. But if the portfolio manager makes a few mistakes, shareholders may suffer mightily.

As you would have guessed, nondiversified funds include a few of the very best performers, a few average performers, and a disproportionate share of the real stinkers. Their betas, naturally, tend to be high. Some funds, by the way, are officially "nondiversified" but nonetheless hold a wide selection of securities.

You can usually tell how well diversified a fund is by checking its R squared, a measure of a fund's diversification. R squared (coefficient of determination) is the percentage of a fund's ups-and-downs that can be attributed to the movement of the stock market itself. A fund with an R squared of 100 is as diversified as the Standard & Poor's 500. (Not surprisingly, Vanguard Index-500 has an

R squared of 100.) A well-diversified fund like T. Rowe Price Equity Income has an R squared of 89; an extremely nondiversified fund like Fidelity Select-Energy, 30.

A fund with a high R squared is typically more stable, and one with a low R squared may be more volatile. But the R squared is not an infallible measure of a fund's stability. Valley Forge is one of the most conservative of all funds; it's really a money-market fund masquerading as a stock fund. Once in a while, it launches a foray into an underpriced blue-chip stock, makes a killing, and quickly retreats. It has an R squared of 19.

Should you ever consider a nondiversified fund? Certainly if it's a fund with Sequoia's glittering record, or if it's as conservatively managed as Valley Forge. (Sequoia has most of its assets in Berkshire-Hathaway, Warren Buffett's company.)

37

INDEX FUNDS

Indexes are replicas of the stock market, or of any other market, as a whole. The most famous index, the Dow Jones Industrial Average, contains 30 blue-chip stocks. As an index, it's crude but useful. It doesn't reflect what is happening among small-company stocks. And it exaggerates the market's movements. The Standard & Poor's 500 Stock Index is preferred by professional investors, but it, too, is skewed toward big-company stocks. Other indexes—the Wilshire 5000, the Value Line Composite—are less well-known, but they give a more comprehensive picture of what the market as a whole has been doing.

Index funds are modeled on a market index, typically the S&P 500. Generally, they perform a little worse than the index, because they have more expenses (it costs money to buy and sell stocks according to their representation in the S&P 500).

Big-company stock index funds tend to do better than 75% of all mutual funds. Bond index funds tend to do better than 80% of all mutual funds. Why invest in anything but an index fund, then? An index fund like Vanguard's 500 is no-load; it has a zero management fee; its expense ratio is a tiny 0.19%; its turnover is low. And its ten-year average annualized return has been 15.7%. Its beta, of course, is 1. And you get extraordinary diversification.

Despite these advantages, most investors are reluctant to invest in an index fund. Perhaps because it's hard to accept doing only average, or because owning an index fund is dull. Watching your fund compete against the averages is much more fun. Finally, for a sophisticated investor, it's easy to resist buying shares of an index fund when there are other funds, like Fidelity Magellan and the Twentieth Century Giftrust Fund that over time beat the S&P 500 by a good margin.

Still, older investors, conservative investors, might think about an index fund. Kevin Johnson, Vanguard 500's former portfolio manager, suggested putting 70% of your stock portfolio into his fund and 30% into more aggressive funds.

While Vanguard's was the first index fund open to the public, such funds have begun to proliferate. There's also a fund that invests in the 10% of New York Stock Exchange issues with the lowest market capitalizations. And even Vanguard has come out with lots of new index funds—of small-company stocks, foreign stocks, value stocks, growth stocks, and so forth.

38

ETHICAL FUNDS

Sometimes mutual funds seem to give investors *too* many choices, and that seems to be the case with "ethical" or "socially responsible" funds.

Such funds may avoid investing in tobacco and liquor companies, companies with nuclear-power plants, companies with strained labor relations, or companies that make weapons.

No two ethical funds seem to have the same "screens." And not much love is lost among the different funds.

The intriguing question about such funds is whether they perform any better, or worse, than other funds.

Advocates of the funds claim that they will always do well. After all, they avoid troubled companies—like those with nuclear power, those that grow tobacco, those with strained labor-management relations.

Opposing arguments: Success in the market is usually the result of buying stocks low—whatever the companies behind the stocks; focusing on ethical investments narrows your investment universe and serves as a distraction.

A simple way to resolve the argument is to examine the long-term record of two of the oldest ethical funds: Dreyfus Third Century (1972) and Pioneer (1928). Both have always been strikingly average performers.

Ethical funds are not necessarily for investors seeking the highest possible returns. Sheldon Jacobs, editor of *The Handbook for No-Load Fund Investors,* dismisses ethical funds this way: "Given their relative unattractiveness, investors might consider putting their money into better-performing funds and giving the additional profits to their favorite charity."

An interesting new ethical fund is Neuberger & Berman Socially Responsive Fund, telephone: (800) 877-9700.

39

NEW FUNDS

Throughout the land, very intelligent and imaginative people are thinking up ideas for new mutual funds. Like a new invention, or a new type of business, a new and truly needed fund can be an avenue to money and fame.

The question is whether an investor should ever put money into a new fund. There is, after all, a powerful argument against it: The new fund has no track record. Yet there are fine funds that have been around for 3, 5, 10, 20, and 30 years.

Certainly you should not buy new closed-end stock funds—their prices almost invariably plummet. You also should be skeptical of new open-end funds, and probably never put any significant amounts of money into them, but you might want to consider such funds under certain circumstances.

1. A successful fund has been closed to new investors but its managers have opened a "clone" fund.

   These clone funds tend to do almost as well, or as well, as their older, bigger models. The new portfolio managers probably have learned at the feet of the masters, and while the two may not buy identical securities, they probably buy very similar securities.

2. The investment company launching the fund has a fine record.

   Many rookie funds that do splendidly during their first years are the offspring of famous families. The companies behind them were probably blessed not just with talent and experience, but a knowledge of what kind of new fund might sparkle.

3. The manager of the new fund has a fine record managing money.

It would surely be tempting to buy shares of a fund managed by such financial wizards as J.P. Morgan or Bernard Baruch. There are many contemporary money managers of great skill. Who could doubt, for instance, that Mario Gabelli would make a success of Gabelli Asset, considering that he has been No. 1 year after year in managing money for private accounts?

Still, one must remember horrifying exceptions: A noted investment adviser, Gerald Tsai, lost a lot of his shareholders' money after launching his first mutual fund in the 1960s.

4. The new fund has a shrewd new approach that fits in with some of your own thinking.

Take the new asset-allocation funds. USAA Cornerstone, for example, shifts its investments among U.S. stocks, foreign securities, precious metals securities, and fixed-income securities—a system many people have come to like. For safety, there are minimum and maximum levels within each sector—so the fund will never be, say, 100% into precious metals. USAA Cornerstone ended the difficult year of 1987 with a total return of 9%.

40

SIZE AND PERFORMANCE

A fund's assets—money under management—minus its current debts (taxes and other operating expenses) make up its net assets.

The net assets of a fund that has been flourishing will usually grow, simply because more and more investors will move into that fund.

Naturally, the best-performing funds tend to be large. (These days, $250 million is considered medium-sized for an aggressive-growth fund, $500 million for a growth fund.) Investors flock to them. But that leads to the intriguing question: Once a fund gets to be large, does its performance suffer?

Generally, the answer of the experts is Yes. Muscle-bound funds cannot buy small issues and make enormous profits—because they would move the price of such stocks too far up. And the large funds are leery of buying into small-capitalization stocks anyway, because if they decided to sell, they would drive the prices down.

Also, a large fund cannot quickly shift its holdings to take advantage of changes. When a $5 billion fund wants to buy $75 million worth of a stock (a typical holding for a fund of its size), it usually can purchase $1 million a day without unduly driving up the price. So the fund may need 75 days to move into a stock—and 75 business days to move out. On the other hand, a small fund can buy small-company stocks as well as large ones—and turn on a dime.

Should you, then, stick with stock funds that have less than $250 million in assets? The answer is No.

If you had followed that strategy in recent years, you would have been very sorry. From 1983 on, blue-chip stocks have been on a tear—while small-company stocks languished during the late 1980s. Blue chips did well because foreigners were more interested in them, and because of the proliferation of index funds, which typically buy the blue-chip stocks that make up the leading indexes.

Besides, the best portfolio managers and analysts tend to wind up at the gigantic funds. These funds become gigantic because of their expertise, and because their employers have huge assets, they are better paid—and they get more acclaim from the public and from their peers.

A giant fund will also have the clout to buy shares of an attractive new issue.

The best reason to consider giant funds, though, is given by Michael Price of Mutual Shares. The more assets you have, the more easily you can afford to hire new analysts in new areas—and the more undervalued stocks you can find. This helps balance things out.

Certainly, despite their elephantine clumsiness, gigantic funds like Vanguard/Windsor and Fidelity Growth and Income continue to do well. One reason is that they can afford a flock of top-flight analysts, and therefore have access to the most timely, reliable information.

With fixed-income funds and money-market funds, you're probably best advised to favor those with the greatest assets. Such funds have more clout and can buy the most attractive new issues. They can also diversify more. On the other hand, if you have a choice between two growth funds with similar records, you should probably tilt toward the one with lower net assets.

41

NET ASSET VALUES

The net asset value, or NAV, of a mutual fund is the fund's price per share. For most money-market funds, for example, the NAV is kept at $1, and $1000 will buy you 1000 shares.

With *no-load funds,* you pay the NAV when you buy shares. If you invest $1000 in a typical no-load stock fund with an NAV of $15, you will own 66.67 shares ($1000 divided by $15).

With *load funds,* the sales commission determines how many shares you will wind up with for, say, $1000. If the load is 5%, $50 of your $1000 goes for sales commissions; if the NAV is $15, the "offering price" would be 15.79 ($15 divided by 95%). You would wind up with 63.33 ($1000 divided by 15.79). Or divide $950 by $15 to get 63.33 shares.

You calculate the asset value by taking the value of the securities that a fund is managing and dividing that figure by the number of shares outstanding. If a fund's net assets are $10 million, and there are 500,000 shares held by investors, the NAV is $20.

The NAV fluctuates from day to day, mainly depending on how the securities the fund owns have performed the previous day. It also fluctuates because of withdrawals to pay fund expenses, and occasionally because of distributions—when the fund passes along capital gains, dividends, and interest to its shareholders.

The actual NAV has little significance to the average investor, though it can be suggestive.

When a fund is first made available to investors, its managers decide on an offering price per share. The number is arbitrary, but usually it's $10.

But when one gold fund was first offered, its price was set at $1—to suggest that the fund was speculative.

A high net asset value, on the other hand, may indicate conservatism. The NAV of Endowments, Inc., a growth-and-income fund for tax-exempt institutions, was once around $1676, just before a 100-to-1 split. When the fund was launched in 1970, the NAV was set at $1000 per share—so that "investors would not think that this was play money," a spokesperson explains.

Beyond that, a fund with a very low NAV may not have performed well—and a fund with a high NAV may have been outstanding. Steadman Technology's NAV was recently $1.12; Fidelity Magellan's, $88.

But this is not an infallible guide. The number depends not only on the fund's performance but also on how long the fund has been in existence, whether the original NAV was $10, and whether or not the fund has ever split its shares (giving investors two shares for the price of one, say, and cutting the net asset value in half).

42

DISTRIBUTIONS

Any money that a mutual fund directs your way is a "distribution," including:

- dividends from common and preferred stocks;
- interest from bonds and Treasury obligations—which, confusingly, are classified as "dividends";
- net realized capital gains—profits from assets that went up in value before being sold, minus losses from assets that declined in value before being sold (*realized* means that the securities were sold; you don't owe capital gains taxes on securities you haven't sold, even if their value has grown);
- tax-exempt interest dividends—you now report them on Form 1040, though they are usually still not taxed;
- return of capital—nontaxable disbursements, because you're getting back your principal (sometimes these distributions are called "tax-free dividends");
- undistributed capital gains—in rare instances, a fund pays taxes on its gains even before selling the securities. You must pay taxes on the gains the fund allocated to you, even though you didn't receive them.

What sort of distributions you will receive from a fund depends on the fund. Aggressive-growth and growth stock funds will bless you, if you're lucky, with mostly capital gains; stock income and fixed-income funds will give you dividends, interest, or both.

Mutual funds normally do not pay taxes on any capital gains, interest, or dividends they receive from their holdings because they disburse almost all of these gains to their shareholders. They are merely a conduit. But to continue to qualify as a nontaxable conduit, during a calendar year they must distribute most of their net realized gains and income dividends.

When you buy shares of a mutual fund, you are asked to make a choice: Do you want your distributions reinvested in more shares; or do you want them mailed to you? Do you want capital gains mailed to you, and dividends reinvested—or vice versa?

Most shareholders—around 80%—reinvest all their distributions. It's a good way to obtain more shares automatically, as well as to practice a rough version of dollar-cost averaging (see Key 49).

In general, it's not a good idea to buy shares of a fund just before a distribution. You will receive part of your investment back—and it will now be taxable. Even if you directed that your distributions be reinvested, you will owe a tax. (But by paying taxes on these distributions, the "basis"—cost for tax purposes—of your new shares will be different.)

Most funds make distributions in December; some also make them in July. Phone a fund to make sure you aren't investing just before a distribution. If you're investing only a small amount of money, though, and you're eager to own shares, you might plunge ahead. The tax liability will usually be small.

43

EX-DIVIDEND DATES

The term "ex-dividend" comes from the stock market. When a stock issues its dividend, its price generally goes down, to reflect the disbursement. Buyers of *new* shares on or after that day aren't entitled to that dividend.

The term has been carried over to mutual funds, but here the term "ex-distribution" would be more suitable. After all, a fund supposedly can go "ex-dividend" when it distributes capital gains as well as dividends.

Some newspaper listings do distinguish between "ex-dividend" ("x") and "ex-distribution" ("d"). In this case, "ex-distribution" means capital gains, or capital gains as well as dividends.

On a fine spring day recently, many newspapers published the following in their mutual-fund listings:

	NAV	Offer Price	NAV Chg.
Nicholas	xd 31.72	N.L.	–.38

On that day, about 300 alert shareholders phoned the Nicholas Fund to ask either, Why had the fund lost so much money? or What was the distribution?

Novices asked the first question; veterans asked the second.

The fund, of course, had gone ex-dividend or ex-distribution. It had parceled out most of its net profits from securities it had sold earlier in the year, along with accumulated dividends and interest. Shareholders who wanted those distributions reinvested now owned more shares, at a price of $31.72 apiece. Those who wanted the distributions mailed to them received a check.

But unless they telephoned the fund, shareholders didn't know what their holdings were worth now or how much money they would receive. They would not know until the following week, when they received a mailing from the fund.

The reason is that the "–.38" was a combination of two numbers. One was for the money set aside for the distribution, representing (as it happened) –.57 of the fund's net asset value per share. The other number was +.19, the amount that the fund's NAV had risen the previous day. Together, they added up to the –.38 change listed in the newspaper.

To learn what their holdings were worth now, share-owners could

- multiply the number of shares they owned before the distribution by 32.29 (31.72 + .57); or
- multiply the new number of shares they now owned by 31.72. The new number is the old number they owned, plus (the older number times .57 divided by 31.72).

Of course, as long as they were phoning Nicholas to learn what the distribution was, they could also ask what their current holdings were worth.

Newspapers get their data from the wire services—Associated Press or United Press—which, in turn, get them from Nasdaq, the National Associated Securities Dealers Automated Quotation system. Nasdaq does provide a breakdown of the change in the net asset value, but newspapers don't use it, claiming that they lack the space. But they could easily print the distributions at the bottom of the listings.

44

MONITORING FUND PERFORMANCE

You can check how your funds are performing from day to day by looking at the Mutual Funds listings in any large newspaper.

But to check how your funds are faring compared with other funds, or how they have performed over a month, three months, or longer, you should subscribe to a mutual-funds newsletter or a financial magazine.

Below is what you are likely to see in a newspaper:

Mutual Funds Fund Family	NAV	Dly % Ret.	YTD	5-yr % Ret.
Acorn				
Acorn d	14.64	+0.5	+7.46	+19.6
American				
Amcap m	14.08	+0.4	+3.0	+12.5
American National				
Growth f	4.57	–0.4	+4.1	10.8
Berger				
100 b	19.25	+0.1	+6.4	+17.9
Berwyn				
Berwyn d	20.79	+0.8	+6.9	+17.9
Columbia				
Balanced x	20.32	–0.1	+2.0	NA

NAV means "net asset value"—the price per share of a fund. A share of Acorn was worth $14.64 on that day.

Dly % Ret means "daily percentage return," how much the fund went up or down the previous day—including reinvested distributions. Acorn rose 0.5%. Multiply that by $14.64, to get .0732. (The fund's price went up a little more than seven cents a share.) Subtract that from $14.64, and you get the previous day's price: $14.566.

So far this year (Year to Date), Acorn's total return has been 7.46%. Over the past five years, it's been 19.6% a year.

The "d" after Acorn means that there's a deferred sales charge or a redemption fee. (In this case, a redemption fee.)

The "m" after American AmCap means that there are multiple fees—a sales charge or redemption fee, plus a marketing fee (12b-1 fee).

The "f" after American National Growth means "front end sales charge."

The "b" after Berger 100 means a 12b-1 fee is in place.

The "d" after Berwyn means there's a deferred sales charge or a redemption fee, in this case, a redemption fee.

The "x" after Columbia Balanced means that the fund paid out a distribution yesterday—interest, dividends, capital gains, whatever. The fund's NAV may have fallen because of the distribution: A fund's net asset value usually declines when it invests its realized capital gains, dividends, or interest on behalf of shareholders, or mails them a check for the money. (The NAV wouldn't decline if the value of the fund's holdings rose so much that they offset the loss of the distribution.)

"NA" means "not available"—the fund hasn't been in existence for five years.

The symbol p (not shown on the chart p. 98) means that the figures are for the day before. (Funds that invest in other funds, for example, are always a day late in reporting their figures.) And s means that the shares have split—if you had owned 20 shares, you now might have 30 or 40.

Some newspapers use different symbols. And some just list the new NAV—you need the listings from the previous day to see how your fund has fared.

To be listed by the National Association of Securities Dealers a fund must have 1000 shareholders or $25 million in net assets. That's why you may not find a new fund listed, even though it may have a superlative performance record.

45

FIGURING OUT
THE YIELD

Your yield usually means the income you can pretty much count on receiving from an investment.

With mutual funds, though, the meaning of the word is a little slippery—and it can be very misleading.

If you invest in a certificate of deposit, you usually get an unvarying yield—say, 7% for a one-year CD. But the yield from a mutual fund of different stocks, bonds, or both will vary continuously, as the individual stocks and bonds go up or down in price.

Here's how the 12-month yield is calculated:

Add all income distributions—dividends, interest, or both, but not capital gains—for the preceding 12 months. Then divide by the current net asset value (minus capital gains distributions). Capital gains or losses aren't part of the yield; they aren't regular or predictable. But they do constitute part of the total return—your yield *plus* gains or losses on your principal.

Before the Securities and Exchange Commission cracked down, some funds were advertising weekly or monthly yields, and some were including capital gains as well as irregular and unpredictable option income. Now advertised yields must be uniform.

Funds with the highest yields tend to hold bonds, high-dividend stocks, or both.

Buying a fund simply because of its high yield can be a terrible mistake. Recall the story about the man who was on vacation, driving across the country. He turned to his wife next to him and joyfully told her, "I'm lost, but—I'm making great time!" With a high-yielding fund, you can be making great time, heading directly for the poorhouse.

When you invest, you don't just want sizable regular distributions; you also want your original investment to retain its value, or even appreciate, and certainly not sink.

A stock's yield depends on both its price and its regular dividend. If a stock's price is $25 a share, and its regular dividend is 50 cents per share a quarter, your yield is 8%. (The dividend is $2 a year; divide $2 by $25.) But if the company's profits begin vanishing, investors will sell the stock. Its price might drop to $20 a share. That means that its yield grows to 10%. This isn't cause for rejoicing: The value of your shares has dropped 20%. And there's a danger that the company, pressed for cash, will cut its dividend. The same is true of the bonds issued by a company in trouble—their prices may sink, and their yields climb.

In short, a big yield can be a sign of big trouble.

The same goes for a mutual fund with a high yield. Its stocks or bonds may be on the fringes of financial stability. A bond fund may own low-rated, "junk" bonds; a stock fund may own issues with a high yield only because their prices are in the basement. Yet a high yield isn't always cause for alarm. A stock or bond fund may have so many different risky securities that some of the overall risk is diversified away.

To determine whether a fund's high yield means that it carries high risk, check its total return, too. The total return takes into consideration what is happening to your principal.

In a money-market fund, a high yield may mean that a fund is efficient; or it may mean that the fund owns short-term instruments with unusually long maturities—and if interest rates suddenly rise, that fund may be in for a long spell of below-average yields.

46

DECIPHERING
THE PROSPECTUS

A mutual fund cannot sell you shares unless it sends you a prospectus. (And if you become a shareholder, it must also send you updated prospectuses.) If you just send in a check asking to buy shares, the fund may invest the money on the day it comes in, sending you a prospectus and an application form when it mails back a confirmation of your investment. (But at least one fund, Lindner, will mail back your check if you haven't submitted an application form.)

The cover of the prospectus usually tells you a fund's investment objective (high income, capital gains, etc.); sales or redemption charges; minimums for first and repeat investments; retirement plans available; address and phone number.

Inside the prospectus is a table of all fees, charges, and operating expenses. The Securities and Exchange Commission now requires funds to show how much these fees and charges cost an investor if he or she redeems the shares at the end of one year, three years, five years, and ten years—assuming a first investment of $1000 and a 5% growth rate (rather low). Usually you'll also find financial statements—income and capital charges per share, expenses, net realized and unrealized gains or losses, distributions, and so forth.

The Investment Company Institute suggests that, in reading a prospectus, you concentrate on

- Date of issuance. Make sure you have the most recent edition (prospectuses must be updated every 16 months).
- Minimum investment

- Objective
- Record of performance
- Degree of risk
- Special features—like check-writing, telephone exchange, automatic investing.
- Fees

Also pay particular attention to the section in the prospectus describing how to redeem your shares. Remember how much you can withdraw by letter without a signature guarantee.

If you request it, you can also receive a Statement of Additional Information, which elaborates on the prospectus itself.

The prospectus is a formidably boring piece of literature. And it doesn't tell you what you probably are burning to know: how this fund has fared over the years in comparison with similar funds. You can get that information by reading a newsletter or a financial magazine.

In fact, if reading the entire prospectus is just too painful for you, you can make do with a description of the fund in updated publications like *Mutual Fund Values, Value Line Mutual Fund Survey,* and *The Handbook for No-Load Fund Investors.* (See Introduction.) Such books will also give you important information missing from most prospectuses, such as who the fund's portfolio manager is and how volatile the fund has been.

Coming soon: a short, easy-to-read version called the "profile prospectus "

47

INVESTMENT MINIMUMS

While a few funds have no minimum initial investment at all—you can even send in a dollar or two—most set a minimum, typically of $1000 or $2500. The minimum needed for subsequent investments is usually smaller— $50, $100, $250.

For novice investors and for the less well-to-do, a low minimum is a help. It's difficult to practice dollar-cost-averaging if you must begin investing in, say, Mutual Shares with $5000. A low minimum is especially suitable for children, to get them into the habit of investing in mutual funds with small amounts.

More and more funds will let you invest a small amount, such as $50, if you promise to mail in $50 a month afterwards.

The minimum for an Individual Retirement Account is usually less than the minimum for an ordinary invest-ment—$250 may be typical. Funds think that IRA money will remain in the fund for a long time, so they encourage contributions. But many funds charge a little extra—$5 or $10 a year—to handle an IRA.

Most funds prefer high minimums, simply because there's less paperwork—fewer mailings, fewer calcula-tions—if the fund deals with fewer shareholders, who own relatively large numbers of shares. Perhaps funds also think that small investors are more likely to sell their shares in a general market decline, thus forcing a fund to sell its holdings at low prices.

Fund families tend to have similar minimums and fol-low-ups. Older funds also tend to have lower minimums.

A no-load fund with a good record and an unusually low minimum is Muhlen Kamp, telephone: (800) 860-3863.

48

BUY AND HOLD STRATEGIES

The most popular strategy for investing in stock and bond funds is to buy those with superior track records (and continuity of good management) and hold on. This tack is opposed to the market-timing approach and to momentum-following.

Market-timers scoff at buy-and-holders. "I invest on the assumption that the following year will be the worst that the stock market has seen for 20 years—and on the assumption that it will be my last year in the market," says market-timer Paul A. Merriman, an investment adviser in Seattle. "So, if the market gives signals of a major decline, it's too risky to remain invested." Merriman got out of the market in 1987, before the crash.

A momentum-follower, Burton Berry, a newsletter publisher in San Francisco, is contemptuous of buy-and-holding: "It's completely out of date. The market is so dynamic and volatile that buy-and-holders will someday wake up and find that their funds are dogs. Their head-in-the-sand belief that long-term records are reliable guides to the future is incredible."

But, as is true throughout the world of mutual funds, the term "buy and hold" is so broad that it can be misleading.

Many buy-and-holders aren't strict buy-and-holders. They would not dream of buying a fund on the strength of a recent fine record, and holding their shares while the fund went into a seemingly permanent tailspin. Most buy-and-holders don't hold on forever.

When do these flexible buy-and-holders sell? When an aggressive-growth fund has underperformed similar funds for one or two years. When a growth or growth-and-income fund has lagged similar funds for two to three years.

Very likely, flexible buy-and-holders also engage in a bit of market-timing. Perhaps they buy funds whose managers tilt toward market-timing—Vanguard Asset Allocation, for example. Perhaps they dollar-cost-average (see Key 49), which is a milk-and-water version of market-timing. Perhaps they follow the formula approach, keeping a certain percentage of their overall portfolio in stocks—raising it when their holdings (and the market) are down, pruning back when their holdings (and the market) are up. Or they may just lighten up a bit when they think the market is high, load up a bit when they think the market is low.

49

DOLLAR-COST AVERAGING

"Dollar-cost averaging" means diversifying the prices at which you buy an investment over a period of time—so you wind up paying average or below-average prices. You try to "average" the "dollar-cost" of your securities.

Mutual funds can help you diversify your overall portfolio and your subportfolios. But it's up to you to diversify the prices you pay for any investments.

If you invest a large sum all at once, you may pay too high a price—and wait a very long time before your original investment begins appreciating. If you had bought Fidelity Magellan on January 1, 1987, by the end of the year you would have been ahead by 0.96%. If you had bought all your shares in early October, by the end of the year you would have sustained a loss of almost 25%.

Many amateur investors buy shares in a mutual fund; they watch in dismay as the net asset value (NAV) slowly sinks; then, when the price finally climbs up to their original purchase price, they sell, breathing a sigh of relief.

Logically, you would think that if you staggered your investments, you would wind up with an average price. The truth is more pleasant. By staggering your investments, you wind up with a below-average price. The reason is that if you invest a fixed sum at regular intervals, when the fund price is low, you will buy more shares.

Let's say that a fund is selling at a net asset value of $15. In three months, the price sinks to $10. Three months later, it climbs to $25. Three months after that, it drops to $20. Add up the prices ($70) and divide by four: The average share price is $17.50.

Suppose that during this same period you buy $2000 worth of shares every three months—133.34 shares at $15,

200 at $10, 80 at $25, and 100 at $20. Divide the number of shares you have bought (513.34) into $8000. Your average purchase price is $15.58—less than the average price of $17.50.

Of course, while dollar-cost averaging can prevent disaster, it can also reduce your winnings. If the shares' price had gone up for the entire year, you would be cursing the notion of dollar-cost averaging. But if the price had sunk, at least your average price for those shares would have been lower than it could have been.

While dollar-cost averaging can be suitable for other types of investments besides mutual funds, it works best for securities that are volatile, but tend to wind up higher over the course of time—like stocks. If you happen to stagger your investments into a mutual fund that keeps going down, you will wind up with smaller losses than otherwise—but losses nonetheless. Dollar-cost averaging is no substitute for choosing a good mutual fund to begin with.

A more sophisticated version of dollar-cost averaging is "value averaging," where you buy more shares when the price of a fund has declined, fewer when the price has gone up.

50

FORMULA INVESTING

An alternative to dollar-cost averaging is formula investing. It's another way of trying to ensure that you buy low and sell high.

Let's say that you have decided to apportion your overall portfolio into 50% stock mutual funds, 35% fixed-income securities, and 15% cash equivalents. Then the stock market soars, and your stock funds now constitute 70% of your overall portfolio. So you sell a portion of your stock funds and apportion the profit among your other portfolios, bringing them back up to par. You are probably better off selling the funds in which you have the least confidence. (You could sell the funds that have made you the most money, but that might not be wise. After all, if the portfolio manager has done well, why not stick with a winner?)

But suppose that your stock funds have declined, and now constitute only 25% of your overall portfolio. Now you sell a portion of your fixed-income securities, and dip into your cash, to bring everything back to 50-35-10 again.

This 25%-up, 20%-down formula is flexible; you could use larger or smaller percentages. But don't use the same percentages—25% and 25%, for example. If the value of your stock funds falls 25%, you're now dealing with a smaller figure, and you would need an increase greater than 25% to bring the stock funds back up to 50% of your portfolio. (100 plus 25% is 125; 100 minus 25% is 75; 75 plus 25% is only 93.75.) So make your downside percentage smaller than your upside percentage. It might be 5% up, 4% down.

Another way to accomplish this task is not to realign your portfolio only in response to set percentages like 25% gains and 20% declines in your stock holdings.

Instead, every three to six months, say, you bring your percentages back into line. If your stock funds are 55% of your overall portfolio after three months, you cut back, for example. If they constitute 47%, you buy more shares. Thus, even when the market is relatively quiet, you will be keeping your portfolio up-to-date at regular intervals.

Reminder: Don't start a formula plan from scratch. Ease into stock funds gradually—either by dollar-cost averaging or by waiting for a period of stabilization after a major market decline.

51

INVESTING
FOR COLLEGE

Shortly after my first son was born, I started putting money into a stock mutual fund that everyone had been praising to the skies. The fund supposedly did well in down markets; it supposedly did well in up markets. Over the next ten years, I invested in it regularly.

When I withdrew my money ten years later, my profit was . . . nothing.

The 1970s, as it happened, was a poor decade for stocks. Besides, the celebrated manager of my mutual fund had up and left a year or two after I had bought in: T. Rowe Price himself.

The lesson is: Diversify. Don't put all of the money that you save for a child's college education into only one fund, even if it has as glorious a record as Twentieth Century Giftrust. Buy a variety of funds—small-company funds, large-company funds, growth funds, value funds, foreign-stock funds.

And buy other investments, too—zero coupon bonds, certificates of deposit, U.S. Savings Bonds—so, if the stock market does poorly for a while, you won't despair. You'll know that some of your holdings remain above water.

The sooner you start investing for a child, the more money you can put into volatile small-company funds. You will have a long time horizon, so, if you have the stamina and sophistication, you can wait out any market declines.

As your child approaches college age, say 14, begin putting some of the money into less volatile investments, like short-term bond funds and CDs. Most investment authorities think you should count on a bear market's lasting for four years. If the market is very high when your child is 14, you should certainly start cutting back—or at least start moving into safer stock funds, such as growth and income funds or equity-income funds. If the market isn't particularly high, or if it's gone down a lot, you might take less money out of the market. In other words, if the market is in the dumps when your child is 14, don't automatically sell.

Most advisers suggest that money for a child be kept in the parents' names, for these reasons: (1) the child may be eligible for more financial aid (money in a child's name counts more against the child than money in the parents' names); and (2) so that the child, upon reaching maturity, doesn't decide to take his or her college money and start a rock band.

Twentieth Century Giftrust might be a suitable, very aggressive fund for a child, as part of a larger, more conservative portfolio. To invest in the fund, you must make an irrevocable gift—you cannot change the beneficiary The minimum first investment is $500. The fund invests in fast-growing small companies, and it's an extraordinarily volatile fund, but its total returns over the years have been worth the volatility: over 20% a year for ten years. Telephone: (800) 345-2021.

Just make sure that it isn't the only investment that your college money is in.

52

INVESTING
FOR RETIREMENT

In salting money away for their golden years, some people are willing to take big risks. "I have 20 years to wait," one person may say, "so I can afford to invest all my retirement money in small-company stocks." Another person may have a different opinion: "I want to know that my money will be there when I need it, so I'll invest conservatively."

The two should listen to each other—you may need your retirement money sooner than you think. And if you retire early, you want to make sure that at least some of your retirement money isn't down deep in a dungeon. If you invest too conservatively—putting too much of your retirement money into Guaranteed Investment Contracts, for instance—you may find yourself being forced to retire later than you thought.

Whether you're putting money into an IRA, a 401(k) plan, or some other retirement plan, bear in mind that whatever money comes out of a retirement plan is taxed as ordinary income, at ordinary tax rates. Such money does not enjoy the more favorable treatment accorded to capital gains—currently taxed at a maximum of only 28% when individual rates can go as high as 39%.

That's an argument for keeping income-producing investments in a tax-protected account—equity-income funds, growth and income funds, along with fixed-income funds. In your personal portfolio you might keep:

- "tax-efficient" funds (like index funds), which have low turnovers and therefore don't throw off a lot of capital gains;

- aggressive funds, such as those that buy small-company growth stocks. These funds may bless you with big capital gains, taxed leniently. And if you have losses on your funds, you can sell them and enjoy a tax-deduction, something you could not do if they were inside a retirement plan.

Of course, if you have only a retirement portfolio, you would want to keep a variety of investments there, including small-company stock funds.

The golden rule is that, as you grow older, you should limit your exposure to stocks and increase your exposure to safer investments, those that produce income that you may need to live on. That can mean fixed-income funds or stock funds that throw off relatively high dividends (typically those that buy undervalued big-company stocks). But if you're wealthy and you're really investing mostly for your children or grandchildren, you can be as aggressive as you wish.

Be sure to follow an asset-allocation model, a guide to what a person of your age should keep in stocks, bonds, and cash equivalents.

A very simple guide: Take your age, subtract it from 100, and keep the balance in stocks. If you're 30, you might keep 70% in stocks. If you're 50, you might be 50% in stocks. If you're 60, 40% in stocks. If you're 70, 30% in stocks. This guide isn't bad, though some people may find it too aggressive.

Others may find that too conservative. A far more aggressive guide is to take your age, multiply it by 80 percent, and put the result into bonds. If you're 30, then 24% of your portfolio should be in bonds, and the remaining 76% in stocks. If you're 60, supposedly 52% of your portfolio should be in stocks. When you're 70, 44% of your portfolio should be in stocks.

Here's a more sophisticated asset-allocation model, intended for someone far away from retirement, proposed by Roger C Gibson, a money manager in Pittsburgh:

- *65% in stocks*: 28% would be in U.S. stocks, of which 14% in big companies and 14% in small companies. Another 22% would be in foreign stocks, large and small, along with emerging markets. Some 10% would be in real estate securities, 5% in gold-mining securities.
- *20% longer-term, fixed-income investments*: 11% would be in intermediate-term bonds, mostly high quality but some low rated; 9% in foreign bonds.
- *15% in short-term, fixed-income investments*: a money-market fund and two or three short-term bond funds.

There's no hard-and-fast rule about exactly when and how to cut back your exposure to stocks as you grow older. On your birthday, you might reduce your exposure to stocks—but only if the market is unusually high. If it's low, or your mutual funds are depressed, consider postponing your reductions for a while.

53

MARKET-TIMING

A fierce controversy swirling around mutual-fund investing is whether or not market-timing works. As is often the case, both sides make good points.

Market-timing means lightening up on certain investments when you think they are about to decline, or have just begun to decline, and loading up on certain investments when you think they are about to go up, or have just begun their ascent. A market-timer in blue-chip stocks, ideally, would have invested in August of 1982 and sold out in August of 1987.

Predictably, there is a continuum of market-timers. Over on one side are investors whose idea of market-timing is to have a mere 10% or 20% of their stock-market investments in cash if they're worried, as opposed to their usual strategy of being fully invested or having only 5% in cash. On the opposing side are the aggressive market-timers, who are 100% in cash when they think that stocks are in, or are entering, a bear market.

Making everything more confusing are the indirect market-timers. When they see relatively few undervalued securities, they stop buying and build up their cash reserves. They claim they aren't market-timers.

Most of the best-performing funds over the years have not been market-timers. Why? One possible answer is that, by staying fully invested at all times, such funds drooped in bear markets but soared in bull markets. Another answer could be that most of the older fund managers, good and bad, have disdained market-timing.

Not surprisingly, funds that claim they market-time, as a group, fared better than other funds during the October 1987 massacre.

Most academicians scorn market-timing. Their studies show that, to make a profit as a market-timer, you must be right 70% to 80% of the time. Otherwise, trading commissions will decimate your returns. They have a point. A market-timer must make not one but two correct decisions: when to retreat and when to jump back in.

But if you confine your investing to no-load mutual funds, you need not fret about commissions and sales charges. And if you are in only the most thrilling of bull markets, like the one of 1982–1987, and are on the sidelines only during the bloodiest of bear markets, you should do far better than any buy-and-holder.

Examples of market-timing funds are certain asset allocation funds. Among those with good records, according to Morningstar, are these:

Fund	800 Telephone Number
Crabbe Huson Asset Allocation	541-9732
Flex-funds Muirfield	247-4170
General Securities	577-9217
Invesco Total Return	525–8085
Vanguard Asset Allocation	662–7447

It should have been obvious that the market was overpriced in August and September of 1987. Price-earnings ratios were quite high (22); dividends were low (under 3%); the ratios of stock prices to book value were astounding—five and six to one for some blue-chip stocks, when one and a half or two is reasonable. It should have been equally clear that stocks were underpriced in 1973–1974, when price-earnings ratios were low, dividends were high, and price-to-book ratios were reasonable.

Even ordinary investors should be able to spot extreme market conditions—to lighten up when the market is reaching its all-time highs, and to load up when the market is in the doldrums. Not to practice a moderate version of market-timing seems positively reckless. And, in practice, it's likely that the majority of successful, experienced investors—whatever they claim—practice a mild version of market-timing.

54

REDEMPTIONS

There are basically eight reasons to consider redeeming your shares:

1. The fund has underperformed similar funds.

   A good guide, as mentioned earlier: if an aggressive-growth fund has underperformed similar funds for a year or two, or if a growth or growth-and-income fund has lagged behind similar funds for two or three years.
2. The fund's total returns don't match its volatility.
3. The successful portfolio manager has left.

   If a fund is a member of a large, respectable family, it may not make much difference if a noted manager departs. The family can probably replace the departed with someone just as good. Recently, though, Govett Smaller Companies suffered mightily when Garret Van Wagoner left.

   Of course, you may not know when a successful manager leaves. Some funds don't identify the names of their managers; others claim that they are run by a team of managers, not just one person. Still, the Securities and Exchange Commission is recommending that all funds identify their managers.
4. You need cash.

   Perhaps there's another fund you want to invest in.
5. The fund's strategy changes.

   If you have invested in a conservative fund, you might be somewhat aghast to find, from a quarterly report, that the fund is now investing in small-company stocks. And you might become worried if the manager announces that he or she is no longer looking for undervalued securities so much as growth stocks.

Even so, such changes may indicate that the manager is flexible—that he or she believes that small-company stocks are where the greater profits will be, or that the current fashion is growth stocks, not undervalued stocks.

6. When you have a loss.

See Key 55: Minimizing Taxes.

7. When your financial situation changes.

You may want to sell aggressive-growth funds and move into income funds, for example, when you near retirement.

8. If the market seems poised to drop.

That brings us to the question of how to redeem your shares.

A fund must redeem your shares by 4 P.M. Eastern time on any trading day after it receives a proper request. The fund can borrow money, or use its cash reserves, to send you your money; it need not actually sell your share of the securities it owns. A fund must send you your money within seven calendar days of receiving proper forms.

Redemption Problems. Many shareholders, when they first invest in a fund, can choose to have telephone exchange or redemption privileges. But that may not help if the phone lines are tied up, or if it takes a while before a customer's representative answers. That happened on October 19, 1987, but it has happened at other times, too.

If you don't have telephone exchange or redemption privileges, you must send in a redemption letter, with your signature guaranteed by a commercial bank, a major brokerage firm, or maybe by a savings and loan association—not by a credit union or a notary public. A signature witnessed by a notary is not acceptable because the notary does not promise to make restitution if the signature turns out to be a forgery.

Another problem is that only about half of all funds now accept signatures guaranteed by S&Ls, though the percentage is increasing. Why the bias against savings and loans? One guess is that the funds' "transfer agents," who handle the paperwork, were once exclusively commercial banks, and they still remain prejudiced against S&Ls.

Most funds will redeem your shares upon a written request, without a signature guarantee—but only up to a certain amount. The amount depends on the particular fund. (With Fidelity funds, it's $25,000.) And some funds will not even reveal what amount of money they will redeem without a signature guarantee.

Here are some ways to get your money out of a fund quickly:

1. Buy into a fund that has a sister money-market fund and that offers a telephone-exchange privilege. That way, you can transfer your account from a stock or bond fund to the money-market fund quickly, and your money-market fund checks will give you access to your money in two or three days.

2. Buy into a fund that offers telephone redemption privileges. But only about 10% of all funds allow this, and usually with a limit—such as $5000.

3. Follow what the prospectus says about redemptions—even if you read nothing else in a prospectus If the fund will redeem $5000 worth of shares with out a signature guarantee, and you want to redeem $9800, send a letter one day redeeming $5000, and a letter redeeming $4800 the next. (It works.)

4. Buy into a fund that will wire redemptions to your bank. The redemption letter you send should include the bank's name, address, and "routing number" (phone the bank to find out), your account number, and whether the account is check ing or savings. The charge is usually $10 or so.

5. Have a redemption letter ready in advance, with a signature guarantee. When you actually send the letter, you can add the date. A commercial bank where you have only a safe-deposit box may guarantee your signature. If your bank is an S&L and

your fund accepts a signature guarantee only from a commercial bank, ask your S&L whether it has a working relationship with a commercial bank that will, as a courtesy, process the guarantee. And while a stockbroker is supposed to watch you sign your name, many brokers will guarantee a signature even if you just mail in a letter.

6. Send your redemption letter by an overnight courier service, such as Federal Express, and ask the fund or its transfer agent to send your check by courier, too, billing you for the extra charge.

7. Open an account with discount brokers Charles Schwab, Fidelity, or Jack White, and have the broker sell your shares. These brokerage firms have computerized links with many funds; with others, they know whom to phone.

A Standard Redemption Letter

Please redeem (number of shares) of my holdings in (name of fund). (Or: Please sell all my holdings in so-and-so fund.) My account number is (number).

Sell the shares I purchased on (date). (If you are not closing out your entire position, you may want to sell particular shares—those you bought most recently, if you want to lower your taxable gains; those you bought a while ago, if there is a fee levied when you redeem shares you bought recently.)

Please send a check for the amount to (your name and address).

Sincerely,

(your name as it appears on your mailings)

55

MINIMIZING TAXES

Of course, taxes should never dominate your investment decisions. But . . .

- If you're thinking of buying a fund (A) with a front-end load, first buy a different fund (B) in the same family. Then sell Fund B. and put the balance in Fund A. You'll emerge with a quick tax deduction. Forget about it if Fund B has a redemption fee or if the two funds have different loads. But usually you can transfer within a family of funds without paying a sales commission. This tactic would be ideal for investing in a fund like Fidelity Contrafund (3% load); you would first invest in, say, Fidelity Magellan (3% load, no redemption fee). You must wait 90 days before making such a transfer.
- Always be ready to sell a fund that has lost you money, and put the balance into a similar fund. If the fund you sold rebounds, your new fund is also likely to prosper; meanwhile, you have a tax deduction. Note that you cannot take a deduction on a security if you sell it, then buy a "substantially identical" security within 31 days after the sale—or within 31 days *before* the sale. But you can switch between mutual funds and not infringe this "wash sale" rule. Rarely are two funds substantially the same, even if one is supposedly a clone of the other. Nicholas and Nicholas II, for example, have very different holdings.

  In fact, some clever investors buy two similar no-load funds, then—before year's end—sell one if it has lost a sizable amount of money. They put the balance into the better-performing fund. They thus enjoy a tax deduction—and move their money over into a fund that's gaining altitude.

- If you want to reduce your holdings in a fund, sell the particular shares with the least gains—ordinarily, the ones you bought most recently. That will lower any taxes you owe for the current year. Of course, if you purchased shares, the fund plummeted, you bought more shares, and then the fund rebounded, you will realize less capital gains by selling the *older* shares.

  If you have overall realized losses in your portfolio, you may again prefer to sell older shares, with greater gains, to offset those losses and perhaps wind up not owing any taxes at all. (You can offset losses against ordinary income, but only up to $3000 a year.)

  Most funds don't send you certificates when you buy shares—unless you request them. So, to make sure the fund sells particular shares, specify—in your redemption letter—the date, price, or date *and* price at which you bought the shares you want to peddle.

- Don't buy shares of a stock fund, as mentioned earlier, just before a distribution. You'll promptly receive some of your investment back, and owe taxes on whatever dividends and capital gains the fund directs your way. Wait until after the fund's ex-dividend date to invest. Most stock funds make distributions in December, but check with the fund.

- If you have been reinvesting your distributions, be sure you use your various purchase prices as your "cost basis"—the cost of your investment in those shares—when you sell those shares and fill out your tax return. Don't make the mistake of using the net asset value of your first investment in the fund. Assuming that the fund's NAV has risen over the years, your new basis for extra shares will have been higher—and thus your profits will be lower, and so will any taxes you must pay.

- Don't forget to add to your cost basis any up-front sales charges you might have been assessed. (Any deferred sales charges or redemption fees you paid will have been subtracted from the amount you realized.)
- If you're thinking of investing in a mutual fund via a tax-sheltered plan—an IRA, an HR-10 (Keogh) plan, 401(k) plan, a variable insurance contract, a variable annuity—bear in mind that you usually cannot deduct any losses you may incur. For tax-sheltered arrangements, consider investing in an income mutual fund or any very conservative fund, then investing in volatile funds for your personal portfolio. That way, you have the option of taking tax-deductible losses.

    Another reason to put conservative funds in tax-protected accounts is that whatever comes out of such accounts is taxed at normal, ordinary-income rates, whereas rates on capital gains are capped at 28%.

    There *is* a way to take a loss on a fund in a tax-sheltered plan, like an IRA. You can make a premature withdrawal. You will pay a tax penalty, of course—unless you're over 59½, or disabled, or you withdraw the money in accordance with your estimated life-span (in other words, as an annuity). But if you withdraw from an IRA in the same year you opened it, you will incur a tax penalty only on any income you've received, not on both your income and your contribution. Compare the size of your tax-deductible loss against the tax penalty.
- If you own shares of a fund that buys Treasury obligations, check with your state tax department to learn whether the income you received from that fund is exempt from state taxes. Some states say yes, others say no.
- For guidance in filling out your tax return, ask the Internal Revenue Service for Publication 564 (Mutual Fund Distributions).

Appendix

TEN KEY DECISIONS YOU MUST MAKE

1. Do you want a stockbroker or financial planner to buy funds for you?

If your answer is yes, choose a load fund. If you want to invest on your own and save on commission costs, choose a no-load or low-load fund. (Note: All money-market funds are no-loads.)

2. Do you want a fund that gives you regular income, or one that may give you even more of a profit, with capital gains?

For income, choose a fixed-income or money-market fund. For possibly greater profit, an equities (stock) fund. For a combination, choose a balanced or stock income fund.

3. What kind of stock fund do you want?

You can choose among many classifications—among them, aggressive, growth, growth and income, and stock income. Your decision will depend on how much volatility and risk you can stand—and how much income you may need.

4. Do you want an all-weather, a fair-weather, or a foul-weather stock fund?

All-weather funds do respectably in both up markets and down markets; fair-weather funds excel in up markets; foul-weather funds do best in down markets.

5. What kind of investment strategy do you favor?

Buying stocks whose earnings are climbing and whose prices rising? Undervalued stocks? Stocks of companies that may benefit because of special situations? Or just index funds stocks that will do about as well as the general market? Choose your funds accordingly.

6. Do you want a fund that market-times?

A fund that practices market-timing—buying or selling depending on the direction of the market—may keep you from losing money in bear markets but may also cause you to miss out on bull markets.

7. Do you want a specialty/sector fund?

You can choose funds that concentrate in a particular industry, like health care, real estate, precious metals, or utilities, or in one part of the United States or one foreign country.

8. What kind of fixed-income fund do you want?

All Treasurys? Treasurys plus mortgage securities backed by the government? Or just mortgage securities? High-grade corporates or high-yield corporates? High-grade municipals or high-yield municipals? International bonds? Short-term, intermediate-term, or long-term? Your decisions will depend on how high a yield you want, and how much risk you can live with. A good choice might be a flexible bond fund, which just tries to buy the best securities.

9. Do you want a fund from a family or a stand-alone fund?

A family is usually more convenient—but don't choose a family member over a similar stand-alone fund with a better record.

10. Once you know the kind of fund you want, how do you find out which funds in that category have the best performance records and the fewest handicaps?

Read this book, giving particular attention to the successful funds listed in many of the keys.

QUESTIONS AND ANSWERS

1. Can you define "mutual fund" in plain English?

When investors pool their money to buy securities, you have a mutual fund. With a large sum, the group can purchase a wide variety of stocks or bonds. The individual investor owns shares of all these securities, in proportion to the money he or she has contributed.

Usually the term "mutual fund" also means the sort of investment company that lets you buy and sell shares directly from the fund. (If the shareholders buy and sell shares from other shareholders, it's a "closed-end" mutual fund.) The term also usually means a company that actively buys and sells securities. (If the securities in the fund aren't traded, but are simply held in the fund for years, it's a "unit investment trust.")

Finally, many people use the term "mutual fund" to mean an investment company that concentrates on buying and selling stocks—not bonds or short-term debt instruments (a money-market fund).

2. Why shouldn't I just buy and sell stocks on my own?

With a mutual fund, you can get an enormous basketful of different stocks for a comparatively small amount of money. For $2500 (the minimum first investment), you could buy shares of Fidelity Magellan, for example. That fund owns about 450 different stocks. And with such diversity, you are purchasing a large measure of safety. One poorly chosen stock won't lay you low.

Besides, with a fund you would have an expert making the decisions about what to buy and sell—and when

Tomorrow, you could hire such investment experts as Michael Price or Mario Gabelli to manage your money.

3. Why shouldn't I just keep all my money in bank CDs? I won't lose a cent that way, and I won't have to become an investment expert.

With a CD, over the years you would be lucky if your money earned more than the inflation rate. You could be losing money and not know it.

But history has shown that the return from stocks outperforms the inflation rate. Of course, you'll have to choose the right stocks or mutual funds, and be prepared for ups and downs in the value of your investment.

4. I know lots of people who have lost money buying mutual funds. Why should I buy any?

Actually, hardly anyone has lost money in mutual funds who has bought a fund with a good track record, then held on for several years. Of course, some people have lost money in funds. But typically they bought when the stock market was high and then sold when the prices went down.

The average stock fund has returned an average of 9% to 10% a year over the years—far better than fixed-interest investments like CDs. The better funds have returned 15% to 20%.

If you want to raise the odds against your losing money in a stock fund, even temporarily, buy a fund that owns bonds as well as stocks—a balanced fund. Or a fund that may buy real estate stocks or precious metals stocks as well—an asset-allocation fund. Or an index fund, which mimics the performance of a market index, like the Standard & Poor's 500.

Or invest in a fund gradually—a set amount every month, every three months, or every six months. That way, you'll help make sure that the prices you pay for a fund's shares are average prices, not unusually high prices.

5. How much money might I make in one year by buying a mutual fund?

The record seems to be about 184% of the original investment. But in recent years 10% to 15% has been average.

6. How much would I have lost in 1987, because of the crash?

Bear in mind that, before October 19, 1987, the stock market had been going up and up. Overall, the Standard & Poor's 500 gained 5.2% in 1987. Most funds made less than that, and some did lose money.

Despite 1987, the average stock fund was up around 10% a year for the three-year period 1985–1987.

7. Where can I go to get advice about buying funds?

You can ask a stockbroker or financial planner.

But buying good funds isn't hard. You can do it on your own. You'll save money. You won't have to pay anyone a fee, and a commission won't be deducted from your investment money. You yourself may also do as good a job as anyone else.

8. Can I get taken by buying mutual funds?

Yes.

You could buy funds that have done poorly in the past—and therefore may do poorly in the future. In fact, some stockbrokers and financial planners may urge you to buy funds with dreadful records, just because they themselves receive sizable commissions from those funds.

You can avoid bad funds (a) by buying funds on your own, funds that don't pay salespeople commissions ("no-loads"), and (b) by checking that any fund you buy has done better than similar funds over the past three to five years.

9. Can you give me the names of three no-load funds with good three-to-five-year records?

Janus, Dodge & Cox Stock, and Vanguard/Wellesley Income. For the latest information on which funds are doing well, check one of the sources named in the Introduction.

10. Is that all there is to it?

No.

You should know a good deal about any fund before you buy shares. For example, some funds don't fare as well as most other funds in a bull market. They may own many bonds as well as stocks. Others may be exceptionally poor performers in bear markets.

Telephone the funds of your choice and ask for a prospectus and an application form. Read as much of each prospectus as you can manage, then consult other sources of information, such as newsletters.

11. How can I tell that a fund is worth buying?

Your single most important guide is that it has a good record—over three years, five years, ten years (if it's been in existence that long).

Examine other criteria as well, such as whether a fund has a high sales charge, a high expense ratio, or unusually high volatility; whether the current portfolio manager is the same person who was responsible for the fund's excellent performance in the past; whether the fund is part of a respected family of funds.

But the fund's track record should be your chief guide.

12. Aren't mutual funds confusing?

They can be, if you try to learn everything about them all at once.

The problem is that you have so many choices. But take it slowly, step by step, and you won't feel overwhelmed.

You can stick to simple choices when you begin investing—balanced funds like Vanguard/Wellington, or growth and income funds like Scudder Growth and Income.

And, as you go along, you can add to your knowledge, a little bit at a time.

13. I want to make a big profit quickly, but I don't want much risk. What should I do?

When you find out, let me know.

14. Is it true that, over the long term, all funds perform about the same?

No.

A few academics claim that the number of funds that do better than average, or worse than average, are just what you would expect by chance. This is merely suggestive; it's not proof. But one academic has gone so far as to argue that people should choose funds randomly, just by throwing darts at a list of fund names.

The fact is that some funds, year after year, do perform well. Others perform abysmally, year after year. And it tends to be the star performers whose managers have clear and logical investment philosophies, while the poor performers have managers whose philosophies are vague and amorphous.

Anyone who thinks chance governs mutual fund performance might logically buy one of the notorious Steadman funds, which have lost money regularly, and avoid Fidelity ContraFund, Mutual Shares, Oakmark, SoGen International, and other stars in the mutual-fund firmament.

15. I just want to get my feet wet buying mutual funds. Can you name one fund for me to buy?

If you don't already have a money-market mutual fund, you could start that way. All families of funds— Vanguard, Fidelity, Twentieth Century, Strong, and so forth—offer money-market funds. Such a fund is like a fancy checking account. You get higher interest, but your checks usually must be for at least $250 or $500.

An unusually safe fund is T. Rowe Price Spectrum Income, which buys other T. Rowe Price fixed-income funds, along with about 20% in a high-paying stock fund. After owning its shares for a while, though, you may yearn for a little excitement.

16. What are the most common mistakes that beginning investors in mutual funds make?

The two most common mistakes may be:
  (a) Selling funds too soon. Too many people buy shares, watch the fund's price per share sink (perhaps along with the stock market as a whole), then sell out. You should give any fund you buy a decent chance.
  (b) Not selling funds soon enough. As a rough rule, if a fund you've bought has underperformed similar funds for a year or two, it's time to replace it. Another alternative is to sell any fund you own that can give you a sizable tax loss, then put the balance into a similar fund with a good record.

17. I just want income—I'm retired. Should I buy mutual funds?

Certainly. You can buy a variety of funds composed of all sorts of fixed-income obligations—U.S. Treasury securities, Ginnie Maes, corporate bonds, municipal bonds, and so forth. Such funds will give you diversification and a manager who, ideally, knows not only how to buy obligations whose return matches their risk, but also when to buy long-term obligations and when to buy short-term obligations. The Vanguard family offers all sorts of fixed-income funds, with no sales charges and with low expenses.

18. How many different funds should I own?

No one really knows but 10 to 15 is common.

You don't want many different funds in retirement accounts because each fund will levy its own yearly fee. And you certainly don't want many funds that have sales charges if, by combining your investments you could have gotten a reduction in the charge. And you don't want to own so many funds that you can't keep track of them.

Still, it makes sense to own shares of a variety of funds that practice different investment strategies—and even to own shares of funds that seem pretty much alike, just to hedge your bets.

19. What sort of investor shouldn't buy mutual funds?

Someone so wealthy that he or she can hire a top-flight money manager directly and get individual attention. Money managers tend to pay special attention to investors with $500,000 or more.

20. What are the drawbacks of mutual funds?

One of them is that you must sometimes make difficult decisions. For example, few if any funds have unblemished records. A fund that hasn't had a poor year would probably have so much money pouring in from investors that its directors would be forced to close its doors to new investors. What if one of the funds you hold doesn't do well one year? Should you count on its rebounding—or might the fund continue to do poorly year after year? Your safest course isn't to wait around to find out. Switch to a similar fund that has been doing better recently.

Another drawback is the difficulty of determining whether a fund really has a good record. What if it has done well for the past year, but just average for the five years before that? What if it performed spectacularly for five years, then did poorly last year?

In such cases you'll have to use your own judgment. But experts suggest emphasizing a fund's three- and five-year records. Don't buy shares of a 90-day wonder; don't buy shares of a fund whose glory days were eight, nine, or ten years ago.

Still another drawback is that funds buy and sell securities; few of them buy and hold. That means that you will have to pay more taxes—and sooner—on your gains from a mutual fund than if you had bought stocks on your own and just hung on. It can be especially annoying to own shares of a fund that has lost you money—yet you've paid taxes on the "gains" the fund has distributed to you.

Ideally, despite your having paid taxes sooner with a fund, you've reaped more gains than you would have on your own. Of course, you needn't worry about this drawback if your funds are in a tax-deferred retirement account. Or if you bought an index fund, which rarely changes its investments.

SUGGESTED READING

Warren Boroson, *The Ultimate Mutual Fund Guide, 19 Experts Pick the 33 Top Funds You Should Own, revised edition* (Irwin Professional Publishing, Burr Ridge, IL, 1996).

——, *Mutual Fund Switch Strategies and Timing Tactics* (Irwin Professional Publishing, Burr Ridge, IL, 1991).

——, *Everything You Need to Know About Investing . . . In Only 40 Pages!* (Record, Hackensack, NJ, 1993).

——, *Keys to Retirement Planning, 2nd ed.* (Barron's Educational Series, Inc., Hauppauge, NY, 1995).

——, *Keys to Investing in Your 401K* (Barron's Educational Series, Inc., Hauppauge, NY, 1994).

——, *The Ultimate Stock Picker's Guide: 24 Top Experts Pick the 25 Best Stocks to Buy and Hold* (Irwin Professional Publishing, Burr Ridge, IL, 1995).

Warren Boroson and Martin Shenkman, *Keys to Investing in Your Child's Future* (Barron's Educational Series, Inc., Hauppauge, NY, 1992).

GLOSSARY

Adviser A company that a mutual fund employs to manage the fund's investments.

Asking (offering) price Price per share of a mutual fund (*see* net asset value), plus sales charges. For funds with no front-end sales charge, the asking price is the same as the net asset value.

Aggressive growth fund A fund that seeks maximum capital gains. It usually remains fully invested in stocks at all times; it buys small, speculative companies and depressed stocks; and it may employ techniques like selling short and using leverage. Aggressive growth funds tend to be especially volatile.

All-weather fund A fund that does well in bull and bear markets.

Alpha Number that measures how well a fund has performed, considering its volatility. An alpha above 0 is considered desirable.

Appreciation Growth in value of an asset.

Asset allocation fund A fund that either keeps a fixed percentage of its assets in various instruments—bonds, stocks, precious-metals stocks, real-estate stocks—or varies the percentages, depending on where the fund managers think the investment markets are heading. A true asset-allocation fund has some investments in inflation-resistant hard assets (precious metals, real estate).

Automatic reinvestment Choice a shareholder can make to have distributions or dividends reinvested in more fund shares.

Bear market Time when stocks (or other investments) keep sinking in value, despite occasional rallies, or when stocks remain at depressed levels.

Beta coefficient Number that measures how volatile a stock or a mutual fund is. The Standard & Poor's 500 is given a beta of 1. A stock or fund with a beta of 1.20 bobs up and down 20% more; a stock or fund with a beta of 0.80 bobs up and down 20% less. Beta is sometimes equated with riskiness.

Back-end load A charge when you sell shares of certain mutual funds. Also called a deferred sales charge.

Balanced fund A fund that invests in both stocks and bonds—typically 60% in bonds, 40% in stocks.

Basic value investing Investment strategy that concentrates on buying seemingly undervalued stocks, based on their price-earnings ratio, price to book value, and other indicators.

Basis point In bond yields, 0.01%. If a bond's yield goes from 10% to 11%, it has increased by 100 basis points.

Bid or **Sell price** Price at which a mutual fund's shares are bought back by the fund. The bid price usually is the current net asset value per share—unless there's a redemption fee or back-end load.

Blue chip Stock of a large, prosperous, well-established company. The 30 stocks in the Dow Jones Industrial Average—including IBM, AT&T, Exxon—are unquestionably blue chips.

Blue-sky law Legislation passed by individual states to protect investors. (A judge once said that one stock offering had the value of a patch of blue sky.)

Bond A debt instrument that pays a regular interest, whether or not the company issuing the bond is making money. Debt instruments are "senior" securities: Their holders must be paid before a company pays owners of its stock.

Bond fund A fund that invests mainly in corporate, municipal, U.S. Treasury securities. Such a fund emphasizes income rather than capital gains.

Bond rating System of grading bonds on their ability to pay their obligations. Standard & Poor's ratings range from AAA (extremely unlikely to default) to D (in default). Moody's ratings are similar.

Book value Total value of a company's assets minus its liabilities, as carried on the balance sheet.

Bottom up Method of investing in which the investor concentrates on buying attractive stocks, whatever the broad trends of the market or the economy.

Broker/dealer Firm, like Merrill Lynch, that buys and sells load mutual funds and other securities to the public.

Bull market Time when stocks (or other securities) keep climbing in value, despite occasional stumbles. Sometimes the boundary between bull and bear markets isn't sharp.

Bullion Gold or silver in bars or ingots, not as coins.

Buy and hold Investment strategy that entails buying shares of stock or a mutual fund for the long term and selling them only in special circumstances, such as after a long-term loss.

Callable Bond that can be paid off by the issuing company before its scheduled maturity.

Cash equivalents Short-term obligations, like Treasury bills.

Clone fund A fund that imitates another fund, which may have become excessively large.

Closed fund A fund that has stopped issuing new shares. Funds close either because they are so large that the managers cannot find enough good investments, or because the manager prefers investing only in small companies, and cannot cope with large amounts of money.

Closed-end investment company A mutual fund whose shares are bought and sold on an exchange or over-the-counter, by investors trading among themselves. A closed-end fund issues only a limited number of shares. *See* open-end investment company.

Commercial paper Short-term notes, issued by corporations, banks, or government agencies.

Common stock Security representing ownership of a public corporation's assets.

Consumer price index Measure of the changes in prices to retail purchasers, as calculated by the Bureau of Labor Statistics.

Contrarian investing Buying securities cheaply when other investors are pessimistic, selling securities dearly when other investors are optimistic.

Conversion privilege Right of a shareholder to switch from one fund in a family to another.

Convertible securities Preferred stock or bond that can be exchanged for another security under certain circumstances.

Current yield Dividends paid to investors, as a percentage of the current price.

Custodian Bank or other institution that stores the securities of a mutual fund.

Date of record Date on which all investors in a security or fund become entitled to receive interest or dividends.

Deferred sales charge Sales charge you pay when you sell the shares of a load fund.

Distributions Payments that a mutual fund makes to its shareholders, from the sales of its securities, from interest, from dividends—or a return of the shareholder's original investment.

Distributor Company that buys shares of a mutual fund and helps sell them to the public.

Diversification Spreading investments over a variety of different securities, to reduce risk.

Diversified investment company Company whose investments are limited to no more than 5% in a single issue, and no more than 10% of that issuer's outstanding securities; at least 75% of its assets must be in varied securities.

Dividends Money (or stock) that a company pays the owners of its stock, usually four times a year.

Dollar-cost averaging Investing the same amount of money at regular intervals, so that when securities are low-priced you buy more shares. A method of diversifying the prices at which you buy securities.

Dow Jones Industrial Average Model for the stock market as a whole. It consists of 30 blue-chip stocks.

Duration A number indicating the sensitivity of a bond or bond fund to changes in interest rates.

Efficient market Theory that all securities are properly priced, and investors will do better than average only in proportion to the extra risks they take.

Equities Stocks, real estate, other assets that an investor owns, as opposed to bonds, where an investor lends money.

Equity REIT A real estate investment trust that concentrates on buying shares of real estate companies. *See* Mortgage REIT.

Eurodollars U.S. currency held in foreign banks.

Event risk The danger that a bond will lose value because of special situations, such as the issuer being subject to a leveraged buyout and acquiring a great deal of new debt.

Ex dividend The time between the announcement of a dividend and the actual payment. During this time, new investors are not entitled to the dividend. *See* Ex distribution.

Ex distribution The date on which distributions from a mutual fund are deducted from its assets. Also called ex dividend.

Exchange privilege *See* conversion privilege.

Expense ratio Measure of a fund's efficiency in keeping costs down. Annual expenses are divided by average net assets, to factor in economies of scale. Even so, large funds usually have lower expense ratios than small funds.

Fair-weather fund A fund that excels in bull markets but gives a mediocre or poor performance in bear markets.

Fixed-income fund A fund that invests mainly in bonds and preferred stock.

Family Group of mutual funds under one umbrella, typically consisting of a stock bond, a bond fund, and a money-market fund.

Formula investing Investing according to mechanical techniques, such as dollar-cost averaging.

Foul-weather fund A fund that excels in bear markets, one explanation being that the fund invests in securities that are already undervalued.

Front-end load Sales commission investors pay at the time they buy shares of a mutual fund.

GNMA fund A fund that invests in mortgage securities issued by the Government National Mortgage Association.

Global fund A fund that invests in both U.S. and foreign securities.

Growth fund A fund that invests in small companies that seem to have bright futures.

Hedge fund A fund that not only invests in securities, but may also sell short or write options, in order to protect itself from losses.

Income fund A fund that stresses current income rather than growth of capital. Such funds may be mainly invested in high-yielding stocks or in bonds.

Index Model of an investment market—stocks, bonds, utilities, health-care stocks, and so forth.

Index fund A fund that attempts to emulate the performance of an index, like the Standard & Poor's 500 or the Shearson-Lehman Bond Index.

Initial public offering Corporation's initial offering of stock to the public. While many stock prices then proceed to rise, others sink—especially the IPOs or closed-end investment companies.

Institutional investor Pension fund, bank, mutual fund, or other huge investor. Today they dominate the stock market.

International fund A fund that invests in the securities of foreign corporations or governments.

Investment objective Goals of a mutual fund, such as long-term capital gains, with income secondary.

Investment grade bonds Bonds rated BBB, Standard & Poor's fourth-highest category, and above.

Junk bonds Bonds rated BB or below by Standard & Poor's. Such bonds are not so safe as investment grade bonds, but they pay higher interest. Also called "high yield" bonds.

Leverage Buying stocks or other securities by borrowing money.

Leveraged buyout Buyout of a company from its stockholders, with the new owners borrowing funds to pay for the purchase, and perhaps saddling the new company with new debt.

Limited partnership Investment group made up of a general partner, who manages a project, and the limited partners, who invest money and whose liability is limited.

Liquidity Measure of how readily an asset can be sold for cash. If an asset can readily be sold, but at a loss, its liquidity is compromised. In this respect, a money-market fund is far more liquid than a stock fund.

Load Commission charge that buyers of certain mutual funds must pay. The load goes to the stockbroker and the distributor, or—in the case of most low-load funds—to the fund itself. Generally, low-load funds charge 1%–3%; medium loads, 3%–6%; full loads, 6%–8.5%. No-load funds sell their shares directly to investors.

Management company Investment company that runs a mutual fund.

Management fee Money that a mutual fund pays its investment adviser; usually ½% to 1% of the fund's net assets.

Market timing Attempting to buy securities near the end of a bear market, and to sell them near the end of a bull market—in other words to buy low and sell high.

Maturity When a loan—or a bond—is due to be paid off by the debtor or by the issuing company.

Momentum following Buying funds or stocks that have been excelling, and selling those that are faltering.

Money-market fund A fund that invests in debt obligations with maturities of no more than a year. To keep the principal unchanging, usually at $1 a share, the fund varies the yield. Banks' funds are called money-market deposit accounts.

Mortgage-backed securities Shares of a pool of mortgages, issued by Fannie Mae (Federal National Mortgage Association). Freddie Mac (Federal Home Loan Mortgage Corporation), or Ginnie Mae (Government National Mortgage Association). Investors receive regular payments of principal and interest from the underlying mortgages.

Mortgage REIT Real estate investment trust that concentrates on lending money to builders and buyers. *See* Equity REIT.

Moving averages Average price of securities, over a few days or several years. The general direction of prices is a key guide used by market-timers.

Municipal bond fund A fund that invests in tax-exempt bonds issued by states, cities, and local governments. The bonds may be short, intermediate, or long term, and they may be high rated or low rated

NASDAQ National Association of Securities Dealers Automated Quotations, a group that provides quotations on over-the-counter securities and on mutual funds.

NASD National Association of Securities Dealers, the group that polices Securities and Exchange Commission rules governing mutual funds and over-the-counter securities.

Net assets Value of a fund's holdings, minus debts, such as taxes owed.

Net asset value Price per share of a fund: net assets divided by number of shares outstanding.

No-load A fund that does not charge a front-end commission. A "pure" no-load also has no deferred sales charge, and typically no redemption fee and no 12b-1 fee.

Offering price *See* Asking price.

Open-end investment company A fund that can continually issue more shares and thus add to its net assets. *See* Closed-end investment company.

Option The right to buy or sell securities at certain prices. A call option gives the buyer the right to buy 100 shares of a specified security at a set price before a specific date—usually 3, 6, or 9 months; a put option, to sell the shares in the same manner. Most buyers of calls think the market is going up; must buyers of puts think the market is going down.

Over-the-counter Market in which securities are bought and sold through dealers, not on the floor of an exchange. OTC stocks are typically those of smaller companies.

Payment date The date when a mutual fund makes distributions. It is usually a few days after the date of record, when distributions are set aside from assets.

Performance How well a fund has fared over a certain time period, usually measured by capital gains, dividends, and interest the fund has earned.

Portfolio Various securities held by an individual or a fund.

Portfolio manager Person or committee that makes buy and-sell decisions for a fund.

Preferred stock Security that pays a fixed return, and whose holders must be paid before the holders of common stock.

Premium Percentage that a security's price exceeds its net asset value per share. A bond paying high interest may trade at a premium.

Price-earnings ratio Price per share of a stock, divided by its last 12 months of earnings (or estimated earnings for the next year). The p/e ratio indicates how popular a stock is by reflecting how much investors are willing to pay for its earning power.

Prospectus Official document describing a mutual fund. It must be furnished to investors.

Quotation Highest bid and lowest offer on a security.

Random walk The theory that stock prices are unpredictable.

Real estate investment trust Company that buys real estate, lends money to real estate companies, or both. Usually a REIT's shares are publicly traded.

Redemption fee Charge a fund may levy, especially if an investor sells shares purchased recently.

Risk Either the volatility of an investment, or the possibility that the investment will lose value.

Risk tolerance Ability of a person to accept what may be temporary losses from an investment.

Sales charge Commission an investor must pay to buy shares of certain load mutual funds or of a limited part nership.

Sector Stocks in one industry.

Secular Long-term.

Securities Stocks, bonds, options, warrants, or other instruments, that signify a corporation's obligations to an investor.

Securities and Exchange Commission (SEC) Federal agency, created in 1934, that administers the securities laws.

Sell short To borrow a security through a broker, sell it, and buy it back later. Short sellers expect a security's price to decline.

Series fund A fund with more than one portfolio.

Signature guarantee   Document in which an investor's signature is warranted as authentic. Signature guarantees may be required before a shareholder can redeem mutual fund shares. The guarantee usually must be made by a commercial bank or national brokerage firm, not by a notary.

Special situation   Stock that is expected to benefit from a new development, such as an important new product or management change.

Spread   Difference between the bid and the offer prices on a stock or bond.

Standard & Poor's 500   Popular replica of the stock market as a whole, based on the prices of 500 widely held common stocks.

Standard deviation   Volatility of an investment, measured by comparing its average price with the degree of its ups and downs.

Top down   Method of investing in which the investor looks at general economic trends, then decides which industries and companies will benefit. *See* Bottom up.

Total return   Profit or loss that a mutual fund has achieved over a period of time, including capital gains or losses, interest and dividends, and expenses. It is expressed as a percentage of the original value of the assets.

Transfer agent   Company hired by a mutual fund to handle its paperwork.

Treasury   Debts of the U.S. Government. The maturities of Treasury bills are up to one year, of notes, two to ten years, and of bonds, ten to thirty years.

Turnover ratio   Trading activity of a mutual fund, calculated by dividing the lesser of purchases or sales for the fund's fiscal year by the monthly average of the portfolio's net assets. Excluded are securities that mature within a year. A turnover ratio of 100% is the equivalent of a complete portfolio turnover.

12b-1 fee   Amount that a fund takes from its assets—and thus from its shareholders—to pay for distribution and marketing costs. Usually .25% to 1.25% of assets. Also called a hidden load.

Unit investment trust A fund that buys a portfolio of securities—usually bonds—and normally holds them until maturity.

Volatility Fluctuations in the price of a security or index of securities.

Wilshire 5000 Model of all stocks, including those on the New York Stock Exchange, the American Exchange, and over-the-counter. The Wilshire is one of the broadest indexes, and includes over 6000 stocks.

Yield Regular income from a fund, expressed as a percentage of the fund's average net asset value, not including capital gains or losses.

Yield to maturity Yield (as above) plus any certain gains or loss on the price of a bond from now until the time it comes due, expressed as a percentage of the bond's price.

Yield curve Graph comparing the interest rates of similar bonds according to their maturities. Usually long term rates are higher than short-term rates. When short-term rates are higher, it is a negative yield curver.

Zero coupon bond A bond sold at a small fraction of its face value. It gradually appreciates, but no interest is paid to investors, who must nonetheless pay taxes on the interest (except for tax-exempt bonds) Earnings accu mulate until maturity

INDEX